1975

This book may be kept

The League of Frightened Philistines

The League of Frightened

Philistines

AND OTHER PAPERS

BY

JAMES T. FARRELL

THE VANGUARD PRESS

NEW YORK

MANUFACTURED IN THE U. S. A. BY H. WOLFF, NEW YORK, N. Y.

TO

GRACE AND DR. JACQUES LEWIS

"Literary men indulge in humbug

only at a price."

VAN WYCK BROOKS

in "The Flowering of New England"

Contents

Preface

THE PAPERS and essays appearing in this volume were selected from a heterogeneous collection of my critical and non-fictional writing of the past fifteen years. Thus it will be obvious to the reader that they were not written as integrated parts of a book, and that in presenting them in book form I make no effort to impose any formal or artificial unity upon them. Whatever unity they may possess must be inherent; it must be a unity that expresses a constant struggle for clearer perspective and for better orientation. In the main, these papers relate to certain general questions that have interested me and with which I have been preoccupied throughout my literary career. Simply stated, these questions are: What is the role of consciousness in society? Hence, what does culture do in crystallizing, in reforging, and in changing consciousness? What, thus, is the function of literature in society? And, conversely, what is the influence of society on literature? These questions, in turn, lead, inevitably, to the additional question: What is the role of the writer?

Needless to say, I make no claim to, or pretense of, having dealt with these questions definitively. (I hope to write of them more comprehensively in the future.) Here I merely present some of my essays for what they may be worth.

In most of the articles such revisions as I made of the originals, which appeared in newspapers, magazines, or books, were negligible. The essay "Thirty or Under," for example, was written in 1930, when I had published only a few articles, stories, and book reviews. In this article I attempted to offer a program-matic statement on what I thought writers of my age should do and say. Printed here, slightly revised, it is intended to provide the reader with a means of objectively testing my own perform-ance in the light of my early dictum.

Substantial cuts, revisions, or additions have been made in a few of the articles. I have somewhat expanded my analysis of Theodore Dreiser's *Sister Carrie* (which appeared originally in *The New York Times*), and I have revised "The Faith of Lewis Mumford" (originally printed in the *Southern Review*) on the basis of his recent work, *The Condition of Man*. Those parts of "The Language of Hollywood" (printed in *The Saturday Review of Literature*) which were theoretical in character and perhaps confusing as originally formulated have been deleted, and other comment and formulations have been added. The essay on the short story, which discusses short-story handbooks, was originally the introduction to a collection of three volumes of my stories. In this I have made a number of deletions in order to avoid overlapping with other of the articles included in this volume. The other essay on the short story included was orig-inally read as a paper at the First American Writers Congress, held in New York City in 1935. All these papers and essays, except "More on Hollywood," have been printed before.

In this preface I wish to acknowledge a number of specific obligations of indebtedness. The greatest is to Professor Meyer Schapiro of Columbia University. I have had many discussions and extensive correspondence with him, some relating to the writers and the problems treated in some of these papers; some concerning French culture, and also the idea of the nineteenth century of freedom of culture. Besides, I attended a series of lectures he gave on nineteenth-century and modern French painting. From all, I absorbed much. I have also had many talks on literature with William Troy, particularly long discus-sions about Dostoievsky and James Joyce. I am grateful to Dr. Morton G. White of Columbia University for having read a rough draft of "More on Hollywood" and for his suggestions, which helped me, I hope, to improve this essay. I am grateful, too, to Mr. Albert Wohlstetter for suggestions concerning the interrelationship of culture and economy. Mr. James Henle of the Vanguard Press has likewise helped in revisions and editing, and I am also grateful to him for many sympathetic suggestions. Miss Evelyn Shrifte of the Vanguard Press helped me to prepare this book for publication, as she has all my books; her aid, not only on matters of arrangement, but also on many details of style, clarity, sense, and meaning has been of the greatest importance, and I am more than grateful to her. Mr. Bernard Perry of the Vanguard Press helped me to re-edit my discussion of short-story handbooks, and I wish to thank him here for his kind assistance. I am grateful to Mr. Robert Van Gelder, editor of "The Book Review" of *The New York Times*, for his sympathetic interest in all the articles I proposed to write for the purpose of revaluating great, important, or prominent works of fiction. For years I had sought to have such revaluations published, but I never could find any editor interested in my proposal, and in the light of this fact I was especially pleased by Mr. Van Gelder's enthusiasm to publish these little pieces. It was the writing of these revaluations of Dreiser, Hemingway, Mark Twain, Dostoievsky, Ring Lardner, and James Joyce that led me to the decision to issue this book. Mr. Van Gelder also offered me valuable editorial suggestions for my piece on Ring Lardner; these are now embodied in that essay. And to my wife, Hortense Alden, who read and reread all these essays, who helped me to edit them, discussed them with me, and offered innumerable suggestions concerning style and contents, my obligations are incalculable. To all these friends I express my gratitude; at the same time it is necessary to add that none of these friends is responsible for what I have said. That responsibility is my own.

A final word. I publish some of these papers and essays fully aware that they might well be expanded into longer articles. In the group of essays listed in the Table of Contents as "Revaluations" this is especially the case. Here I attempted to set down impressions of books I had read, liked, and been influenced by after I had reread them years later. These essays are

studies of specific books, but not of the full work of the writers
I discuss. It is unlikely that I shall ever get the time to write
long and detailed studies of many writers, and because of this
I deem it best to publish those studies I have already made.
There are fairly severe limits of time for criticism in the life of
a busy novelist, and these papers were written within those
limits. The major portion of my working time for many years
has been devoted to fiction, and these non-fictional pieces are,
in the main, offshoots of this activity.

If, with them, I can contribute toward the clear and sharp
posing of questions and the stimulation of discussion, polemics,
and an earnest desire for clearer perspectives, I shall feel decidedly gratified and amply repaid for my effort. In such a
spirit, then, let me present this collection.

                                            JAMES T. FARRELL

March 22, 1945
New York City.

The League of Frightened Philistines

The League of Frightened
Philistines

*The bourgeoisie has stripped of its halo every occupation
hitherto honored and looked up to with reverent awe. It has converted the physician, the lawyer, the priest, the poet, the man of
science into its paid wage laborers.*—THE COMMUNIST
MANIFESTO, by Karl Marx and Friedrich Engels.

MANY CRITICS and commentators write as if modern culture
were truly organized on the basis of the great ideals of the
Enlightenment. They write as if there were a really free market
in which cultural productions circulated, and as if the dominion
of the mind and of art were one where free minds met and accepted or rejected ideals, art and ideas on their merits. But the
fact is that the free dominion of the mind and of art has never
been achieved in capitalist democracy. Generations of the bold-
est and most honest artists and thinkers have had to struggle,
even bitterly, to maintain their freedom and independence.
However, in most periods of the fairly recent past the area of
freedom in this dominion was larger than it is today. For instance, it was certainly larger in Restoration France than it is in
modern America. And today that already restricted area of freedom is being continually narrowed. As a result, the independent
artist today, in order to be as free as were most of his predecessors, must struggle more uncompromisingly and take greater
risks than they had to.

Correspondingly, we have witnessed how increasing numbers

3

of intellectuals and writers have been turned into real or virtual
wage laborers. Mere employees, these intellectuals and writers
may dare to express what they think and feel only if their
thoughts and feelings coincide with what their employers pay
them to think and feel; at least, they must not express anything seriously and disturbingly at variance with what these
employers like. The stamp of employee is being placed on much
of the cultural production of the times. And many other writers
who formally are not wage laborers have already accepted
the narrow level of freedom of their wage-earning brothers:
they, also, write like employees. An illustration of this condition that can be cited is that of much current book reviewing.
One of the dismal ironies in reviewing, looked at in this light,
is to be seen in some of the bitter attacks launched by so-called
"critics" against writers who have struggled and taken all
the necessary risks to prevent themselves from becoming hired
writers. Reviewers of this type, and with characteristic "originality," sometimes even condemn independent writers as blind
determinists who deny free will and the dignity of man. Can
insolence go much further?

Such reviewers are now deriving their inspiration—if such
it may be called—from those critics who, especially since the
onset of the war, have been conducting a campaign against
a majority of the realistic and advance-guard and experimental
writers of modern times. Also, they sometimes express themselves in apoplectic accents against Rimbaud, Baudelaire and
other great nineteenth-century writers.[1] Needless to say, these

[1] Mr. John Chamberlain, who wrote a farewell to all reform of bourgeoisie
society during the depression, recently remarked in a book review that Flaubert's
Madame Bovary slandered the French bourgeoisie. For many years Mr. Chamberlain defended liberal and radical writers; now he praises the latter-day fulmina-
tions of Mr. Van Wyck Brooks. Mr. Chamberlain has often confessed that what
Mr. Brooks once had to say about America's coming of age helped Mr. Chamberlain himself to come of age. The passage of time has not altered much here,
other than the views of Mr. Brooks and Mr. Chamberlain. It appears that the
latter-day writings of Mr. Brooks have helped Mr. Chamberlain to attain what
is normally called maturity. Now when Mr. Chamberlain writes about literature,
instead of Horatio Algers in the flesh, he sounds like the pupil popularizing
the master. Today he is one of the group that is attacking serious writers.

critics do not discuss those vulgar details of economics which have poisoned so much of modern culture: abstract dignity is their realm.

These men have taken their stand on the unshakable conviction that man does not live by bread alone. For reasons utterly unknown to me, they seem to be of the opinion that many naturalistic and realistic writers want men to do nothing but gorge on bread. When the facts do not convince these men, I do not know how they can be convinced; then they can only be exposed. However, I might remark that some of the writers who have earned the disfavor of these critics have written works which rather persuasively suggest that when men have no bread to eat, or at least do not have enough of it, they live very badly in both the physical and the moral realm. But when one demonstrates this too clearly, it seems that one thinks human beings are as will-less as rats in a trap.

Arguments like this are not new. They have been ignored by every generation of realistic writers for decades. In essence, these Philistines are merely picking up just where the late Irving Babbitt and the late Paul Elmer More left off after they had arrived at exactly nowhere. The language used is a little different from that of the Humanists, and, unlike the latter, many of these critics regard themselves as liberals: Van Wyck Brooks even calls himself a socialist. If anything, Babbitt and More were far superior to Brooks, MacLeish, J. Donald Adams and others of this numerous tribe.

The pasts of these men differ. J. Donald Adams has always been a literary conservative; Van Wyck Brooks, in his earlier days, was a sentimental liberal; Archibald MacLeish has gone through an almost bewildering series of changes. Brooks and MacLeish have higher literary reputations than Adams. But today they have all found a common ground. Here I am concerned not with their differences in the past but rather with their similarities in the present. The fact that these similarities exist and that these men find a common ground here and now cannot be disputed. On one hand, Brooks and MacLeish have

shifted earlier views to the point where they have come closer
to Adams, and where all of them preach in terms of what can
be called a critical cult of responsibility. On the other hand,
Brooks—who has always been unsystematic—has gone through
an evolution as a cultural nationalist and today is a cultural
chauvinist.

To continue, though many formal differences can be found
between these men, and their true predecessors, the literary
Humanists, the latter, among other things, were openly and
admittedly reactionary. But in essence they are performing
parallel services in different periods. And stale as were Babbitt's
ideas, one at least knew what he meant. With some of these
later critics, one must dredge and sweat over their words in
order to find any sense whatever. And then Babbitt far
surpassed Brooks in the talent for compiling quotations sys-
tematically. It is true that More was blind to almost any book
if its author were alive, but at least he could understand some
of the books written by authors who were no more. And he
could write essays of critical merit. Can Brooks, can these others,
write as well on anything as More did, say, on Crabbe? Yes, I
rather yearn for Babbitt and More. Were they alive, perhaps
they could give these critics a clearer line. That would be some
help, at least for their adversaries.

Concerning this new group, read their articles, their speeches,
their books. They sometimes fight "invisible" wars in an "invisible world." [2] Like Napoleon on the battlefield, Archibald Mac-

---

[2] If one reads the mutual praise which men such as Mr. Brooks, Lewis Mumford,
and Waldo Frank bestow on one another, one begins to think that, whether
or not it be a fact that they constitute a literary coterie, they often write of
one another as if this were so. Their writings and that of Archibald MacLeish
have much in common. MacLeish deals in rhetoric and assertions that stress the
same points as do these others. Brooks's Spenglerian notions of literature and
the soil, his ideas of moral regeneration, through literature, these and similar
notions of his are definitely similar to the idea of the "organic" which is
analyzed in *The Faith of Lewis Mumford*. Together, these critics form a national
liberal school of cultural commentators; the emphasis, however, is on *national*,
not liberal. In a sense, MacLeish has joined them in their anti-empiricism.
His speeches, since the onset of the War, tend clearly to separate fact from
interpretation of fact. The interpretation of fact is the abstraction—"the Word."
This is then endowed with a moral connotation, but it is a generalized one.

THE FRIGHTENED PHILISTINES 7

Leish marshals a mighty cavalry of words that he sends charging against the barricades of the intellect and storming the citadels of belief. In the same speech in which General MacLeish performs this mighty verbal military operation, he criticizes modern writers because they are artists trying to tell the truth rather than generalissimos of the simile waging irreconcilable warfare in some unseen world which MacLeish himself confesses he really knows nothing about. Or J. Donald Adams. He has now discovered that God is a principle of literary criticism. But how different is God in his writing from the Almighty of the great religious and scriptural writings of the past. The God of "Genesis" created the entire universe in seven days: the God of J. Donald Adams has not even learned how to understand a good book in more than eighteen years. Such are the critics who have declared open hunting season on writers.

At the risk of wearying my reader, I cite some of their charges. According to Van Wyck Brooks, many writers (including Faulkner, Hemingway, Dos Passos, myself) have been engaged now for years in kicking and tearing civilization itself to pieces. (If this war achieves nothing else, at least it will have saved human civilization from four American novelists.) To continue, writers have no faith in the family (even when they support and love their families); they have no roots in the soil (even though they could not afford to buy soil in order to get these roots); they do not seem to like the idea of running for public office. And, of course, they are irresponsible because they are true artists and tell the truth. And they do not believe in man and in his dignity. They are totally without faith. They *live* and *write* because they are motivated by the death impulse. They are unpatriotic. They demoralized the entire American nation to such an extent that it was totally unprepared to fight

The underlying emphasis here is that of personal regeneration as something separable from, and more important than, social change. Moral regeneration, sometimes considered as becoming an "organic" personality, is conceived unhistorically. This, in turn, is made the basis of developing the idea of responsibility. And responsibility here is really abandonment of a critical spirit. As my analysis of Mr. Mumford should demonstrate, the attack on realistic writers is merely one aspect of a general war of obscuranticism!

a visible war against Hitler, Mussolini, and Hirohito, and one or more "invisible" wars against the barricades of the intellect. These, and sundry other accusations, could possibly make Danbury prison the literary capital of these United States if Attorney General Biddle should happen to read this "criticism" and take it seriously.[3]

Substantially, these charges boil down to platitudes, misrepresentations, impressively irrelevant quotations, petulance and mere unintelligibility. But they are not without their logic. These critics iconize great writers of the past, and ask us to kneel before the icons. In other words, Brooks and his fellow heroes borrow the reverent awe which we give to the great men of the past and use it as a means of blinding people to present realities, not only in letters but also in life. At the same time, they superimpose life in general over modern society in particular; dignity in the abstract over the lack of dignity permitted here and now in particular; morals that are above time over the real character of morality we call the present. By doing this they have high-minded reasons for showing moral density toward the evils of their own day while they disparage that body of writers, living and dead, who have seriously criticized their times. They seem to have little time for denouncing the meretricious art that is written for money and that now deluges the entire nation in an ocean of banality, which is almost unprecedented in all human history. Here, though, J. Donald Adams is an exception: he finds a healthy if immature trend in the sales figures of Lloyd C. Douglas's novels. These men are spiritual expropriators. They have snatched what little they can understand from the great writers and novelists of the past,

[3] Continuing this campaign, Mr. Bernard DeVoto this year entered the fray. His book, *The Literary Fallacy*—which reads as if it were written by a miscegenation of ghosts of Daniel Boone, Pocahontas, Jay Gould, and Evangeline—was a stern defense of the ideas of the frontier and the wilderness. Too bad that it was ex-post history. DeVoto described most modern American writers as unpatriotic and lacking faith in the dignity of the individual, but it also seems to be his idea that the writers who would have ruined America, if the call of the wilderness did not live in the American heart, were themselves ruined by an unpatriotic New Englander named V. W. Brooks. But let us not persist in dealing with farce.

ripped that out of all historical context, and now use it as the rationalization for a morality that can only be called false. Armed with such a morality, they attack those writers who have written about and protested against the evils of their times. They dare not meet one armed with a morality based on the real practice, in culture and in life, of these times. That moral practice is too indefensible: it drips too much with exchange value.

It is the best in these writers—the best in Faulkner, Hemingway, Dos Passos, Dreiser—which these critics attack. Some of these charges, at least, are rendered farcical because of the fact that a number of the writers attacked, directly or by implication, have more or less adapted themselves and are closer to their critics than many imagine. The mood of most writers these days is one that inclines them to surrender, in whole or in part, to the views of their critics. The work these critics attack was written in a spirit of freedom and independence, written without compromise to those bourgeois tastes which reward an author with royalties at the price of honor. If some of this writing sold very well, that was not due to compromises on the part of the authors. Realists have assessed the cost of bourgeois society in terms of what happens to people. The determinism which they have revealed is, in essence, the determinism of social forces and social laws that prevent men from achieving their aims and ends. If these critics are serious, why don't they fight to change these social laws rather than condemn those who help to make us conscious of them. There is no more blind determinism in the operation of social laws than there is in the laws of physical science. What really troubles is not determinism; rather, it is the revelation of what happens to people, the revelation of social tragedy. They also attack symbolist poets of the past and advance-guard writers of our era who have expressed the doubts, the anguishes, the agonies in the psyche of man. There are differences between the naturalists and the realists, on one hand, and between the symbolists and their advance-guard heirs on the other. But both these tendencies are lumped together and misrepresented in this new campaign. And both realists and advance-guard writers have written in a kind of warning, a warning that much is wrong, morally wrong in this world. But the Philistine wants to talk about morals, not to understand what is morally wrong, let alone correct it. Now that these critics have said all they can of Dreiser, why don't they go to work on the morals of financial tycoons like those of whom Dreiser wrote? Now that they have exploded about the "perversity" of Faulkner, why don't they pay some attention to those Southern reactionaries who gained so much from the preservation of the decay Faulkner has described? Serious moralists do not merely abuse writers. They fight the evils they see in their own day and age. These men are not moralists— they are sheep-herders. Their social role is to be mere shepherds for the status quo. This means that wherever there is freshness, sincerity, independence in writing, that is where they must go and try to build a new sheepfold.

And as for this religious trend that is now hailed—where is it? In the books? Don't call that religion! Most of it is mere religious linguistics. Where in it is there real religion, religion to inspire one? Where in it can you find that energy of mind of Augustine, the intellectual scope of Aquinas, the anger of Luther, the consistent if bleak logic of Calvin, the wonderful love and gentleness of Saint Francis, the womanly dignity and intelligence of Saint Teresa, the soldierly ability and genius of Ignatius, the simplicity of devotion of Thomas à Kempis, the real gentlemanliness of Cardinal Newman, the burning sincerity and indignation and exquisite pride of Leo Tolstoy? Where? If one has known religion, and known it, too, in rejecting it, one is not impressed by morals which masquerade as religion, moral density based on fear of living in the present and facing the future.

In conclusion, let me address these gentlemen directly, in my own name and in that of writers and others who will share my views. If you have nothing more to offer, then our battle is won. By yourselves, you are powerless. You are important solely because there is power behind you, the economic and police power of this society. Come out in the open and on the real plane of social morals, wearing your proper uniforms—those of ideological policemen, with a literary star on your blue coats. Neither you nor the power that stands behind you frightens us. Gentlemen, it is clear—you are the league of frightened Philistines. Frightened Philistines can never be masters of the future.

And it is time that you be informed that there are writers, and I am confident that there will always be writers, who will teach you that they can and will defend their convictions. And they will defend, too, the memory of the great writers—Joyce, Proust, Baudelaire, Rimbaud. Yes, power may stand behind you gentlemen, power and the praise of bourgeois Philistines. But we have something that it will never give you. Confidence, confidence and convictions we are willing to defend. The time has come for all of you to join with Van Wyck Brooks in sighing for a new Augustine to write a new *City of God*. You can have that. You will never understand the best of him, but he can teach you something; at least, he can teach you how to be real honest-to-God heresy hunters. We do not need any of that. For we stand convinced that some day there will yet be built a real City of Man. And that is our ideal, that is our faith, that is our conviction. Get down on your knees, gentlemen, and pray, pray for an artist who will be like Lloyd C. Douglas, only an artist. When men learn to have convictions about the future which they know no power on earth can ever shatter, when they believe in a future they know will one day be created, they need none of your "religious" consolation. Some of you are fond of closing books with the sentence: "*Allons, the road is before us.*" *Allons, messieurs.* We, too, will march that road. And know it now once and for all, you will be opposed every inch of that road.

1944

Dreiser's Sister Carrie

Sister Carrie was finished in May, 1900. It has become one of the most historic books in modern American literature, and its widespread acceptance as an American classic marks a major victory that has been won for American letters against the Philistines. With this first novel, Theodore Dreiser demonstrated that he was head and shoulders above the contemporaries of his own generation. No other writer in America during the present century has exerted so great a moral force on his successors. No other novelist has done more than Dreiser to free American letters.

His most serious and bitter struggle came with *Sister Carrie*. Thanks to the enthusiasm of Frank Norris, it was accepted by a major New York publishing house. According to the story of this event related now, however, the manuscript was read by the wife of one of the partners of that firm—a social worker interested in moral uplift. To her, the novel was immoral because the heroine did not suffer "the wages of sin." She insisted that it be withheld from publication. Dreiser, urged on by Frank Norris, demanded that the publishers fulfill the contract they had signed with him. A lawyer advised the firm that, while they had legally committed themselves to printing the book, they were under no obligation to *sell* it. They printed *Sister Carrie* with the intention of storing it away in a cellar, but Norris did send about a hundred copies to reviewers. Some years later *Sister Carrie* was republished and placed on sale and Dreiser once more was denounced as immoral. Concerning the position of the

12

American novelist in that period, Dreiser himself has written:

"I think it nothing less than tragic that these men, or boys, fresh, forceful, imbued with a burning desire to present life as they saw it, were thus completely overawed by the moral hypocrisy of the American mind and did not even dare to think of sending their novel to an American publisher. . . . You couldn't write about life as it was; you had to write about it as somebody else thought it was—the ministers and farmers and dullards of the home."

But Dreiser won his battle, and today he is a living American literary tradition. He helped to raise American life, its contrasts of grandeur and misery, its streets and cities, its tragedies and its vulgarities, to the level of world literature. Such, briefly, is the general significance of Theodore Dreiser in twentieth-century American writing.[1]

[1] At the present time circumstances prevent me from attempting any expanded analysis of Dreiser's work in relation to the writing that immediately precedes him. This is a task I hope to fulfill in the future. Then I hope to discuss his work in relation to that of his important contemporaries and immediate predecessors. Here I wish mainly to make one remark. Dreiser's writing, as a whole, reveals a probing effort to identify social forces, to grasp them, and then to correlate them with human destiny. This is one of the aspects of his work that somewhat differentiates him from such of his predecessors as Henry James, Stephen Crane, and Harold Frederic. In Henry James, a major motif is awareness. Awareness, self-discovery, is also central in Stephen Crane's *The Red Badge of Courage.* Harold Frederic's *The Damnation of Theron Wave* likewise deals, in terms of tragedy, with the theme of awareness. His minister, Theron Wave, gains a sense of values superior to those of a rural, Protestant New York community. These superior values are represented in a doctor who embodies an attitude of science, in a girl whose views are those of the *fin de siècle* esthetics of Europe, and in a priest who represents a sophisticated and liberalized interpretation of Roman Catholicism as a civilizing traditional stream of attitudes and ideas. But the Damnation of Theron Wave results from the fact that he is incapable of assimilating and developing in accordance with the values and attitudes he senses in these three figures. A European and a decayed, rural American pattern of life are juxtaposed in terms of characterizations. Dreiser, as contrasted with these three writers, is most clearly seen as a point of departure. His determinism, more emphasized in *The Financier* and *The Titan* can be analyzed as embodying two important elements: (1) He accepted as science generalizations based on the ideas of nineteenth-century materialism. From these he adduced a deterministic idea, and this, in turn, was represented as biologic determinism. In *The Financier* and *The Titan* this biologic determinism is usually explained by the word "chemisms." Paradoxically enough, Dreiser's appeal to "chemisms" is made quite frequently in specific contexts concerning motivations of characters, where

But how does his first novel read today? Is it merely a novel of historic significance, or does it retain its value now, so many years after it was written?

Sister Carrie is saturated with the life of America during the eighteen-eighties and the eighteen-nineties. It truly re-creates a sense of an epoch: it is like a door which permits us entry into the consciousness of an America that is no more. But it is no mere document. It is a powerful and tragic story, created with an unrelenting logic. Dreiser was so far ahead of his time that his first novel is just as fresh and alive today as when it was written. Many will disagree with me here. Dreiser's style has often been condemned. I myself do not find it so disturbing as do many of his critics. That his writing is uneven, is marred by clumsy passages, is verbose, and is careless and sentimental, I grant. Dreiser obviously concentrates on details rather than on style. He is one of those writers who is more important for what he says than for how he says it. In *Sister Carrie* he often relies on the clichés of the time; this is noticeable in the chapter headings. At the same time, he has moments—passages in which there is eloquence and beauty. Mr. Dreiser's style clearly suggests that he is a self-made writer. A man with little formal education, he had to discover things for himself. He sought to grasp and to represent what to him was an American chaos, and he reflects this in his style as well as his content. Beauty, tragedy, pathos, rawness, sentimentality, clichés—all are smelted together. In connection with his work, one can use the word

we can now see that the real rationale of these motivations can be most satisfactorily explained by Freudianism. Often his "chemisms" are overall generalizations of impulses of which the character is not aware. In this respect Dreiser asserted a biologic determinism, which, in terms of our present state of knowledge about man, is crude. (2) The other and decidedly more important element in Dreiser's determinism is social. He sought to grasp the working and operation of social laws as they effect human fates. His critics often fail to analyze his determinism; they fasten on his generalizations and interpret his work on the basis of these generalizations. And they oppose to such deterministic generalizations moral and philosophical banalities about free will that are mere commonplaces, commonplaces that are usually derived from a false posing of the problem of free will and determinism—as if this were *really* an *either-or* proposition. Dreiser can be described as the American novelist who reflected *social-Darwinism* in his work.

"forged"; he wrote his novels as if he were "forging" images of American life. He took the chaos he saw and out of it tried to build an image of life. To me, there is a raw beauty in his very effort.

Furthermore, though the fact has often been overlooked, there is even a logic and a point for his reiterated moralizations that are included in the narrative: they are not always irrelevant, as many critics have maintained. In order to appreciate *Sister Carrie* in our time it is necessary to appreciate it against the background of its own time.

Dreiser has told the story of his life in other books, and we know how he came to Chicago—callow, eager, hopeful, brooding, with little education, anxious to get ahead in life. He saw the spectacle of luxury in American life sharply contrasted with that of dire poverty; he perceived how eyes blinked at misery and how moral hypocrisy was rife. It was not merely natural for Dreiser to moralize about the panorama he saw: it was practically a subjective necessity. Dreiser's moralizations, on the subjective side were the beginnings of thought, feelings, perceptions, which led him to write the novels that have now become part of a literary tradition.

Objectively, when he wrote *Sister Carrie* it was not sufficient for him merely to have told her story as it might be told now, in 1943. In 1900 it was necessary for him to argue Carrie's case, to defend her, to defend his very right to present such material in a novel. It was essential that he break down the reader's resistance to a realistic and tragic story, in order that it might be received on its own merits. There is a logic and a place for his comments, his moralizations, his asides. They belong to the warp and woof of the period he described and in which he wrote.[2]

---

[2] The naturalism of Flaubert can be juxtaposed to that of Dreiser, not merely in terms of a narrow notion of style and method but, more importantly, in terms of broad treatment. Flaubert is intensive; Dreiser is extensive. Flaubert writes with concentration, with a sharp eye for detail, and with an extraordinary power of suggestiveness. Dreiser generalizes, explains, argues, points out; he lacks Flaubert's power of concentration. This difference is not merely one of art, or of artistic skill. It is social and cultural. Flaubert could be intensive and could con-

In *Sister Carrie* money plays a central role. Without money —money as we know it in our society—the story is meaningless and the tragedy is forced. In order to understand the book clearly it is essential that we understand the all-important role that money plays in it.

To the characters, money is a mystery, as it remains to many up to the present. The good-natured salesman, Drouet, discovers that money comes easily. He sells goods. An order is signed. In time, he is paid a commission. It comes almost effortlessly—and is spent accordingly. To Carrie, a poor and yearning country girl going to Chicago, money is the means for getting everything in life for which she aspires. To Hurstwood, in his pleasant and established life, money at first is not even a problem; later it is the instrument that will permit him to satisfy his passion for Carrie; in the end, it is the means to keep his body and soul together—and he must beg for it on the street.

Dreiser's general comments have often been criticized, sometimes justly, because of their lack of validity. But Dreiser was so much clearer about money than most of his contemporaries that one should remark on this. In *Sister Carrie* he writes: "The true meaning of money yet remains to be popularly explained and comprehended. When each individual realizes for himself that this thing primarily stands for, and should be accepted as, a moral due—that it should be paid out as honestly stored energy and not as usurped privilege—many of our social, religious, and political troubles will have permanently passed." Dreiser came very close to a true and clear definition of money when it is to be considered as other than a medium of exchange —that it is congealed labor power. His clarity, his conscious-

centrate—thanks to the high level of French culture that was his inheritance. Dreiser's cultural inheritance was relatively negligible. Just as he had to discover for himself, so his sympathetic readers similarly had to discover. This extensiveness of Dreiser's method was not preconditioned solely by the hypocrisy of Philistines; it was further preconditioned by the fact that more sympathetic, more alert persons, also had to discover the meanings of American life. The consequences of important economic and social developments are not felt and clarified fully and immediately. They must be discovered temporally. In this sense, the extensiveness of Dreiser's method has a social rationale behind it. It reveals a process of self-discovery in American life.

ness of the role of money, his refusal to be deceived by the mysteriousness that shrouds the definition of money in the popular consciousness of his time, must be grasped if we would understand his work. For no modern American writer has so well dramatized the meaning of money in individual lives.

Above all else, the reason why *Sister Carrie,* to this day, remains so meaningful, so moving and so compelling a novel is Dreiser's portrait of Hurstwood. In Hurstwood, type and individuality merge so well that they are practically indistinguishable. Hurstwood is actually a social function, a kind of glorified major-domo. His entire life flows out of and around his position as the manager of an elegant saloon in the Chicago of the Eighties. What seems to be natural sophistication, manners, *savoir-faire,* is clearly related to his character; Hurstwood's occupation has so firmly molded his character that in his slow, painful, tragic degeneration, the effects remain. From beginning to end, we see in Hurstwood an unfaltering logic.

Here is a character who is all of a piece with himself, with his work, with his station in life. Dreiser understood this man, spiritually and socially; in his creation of him there is perceivable a remarkable unity between the individual and the effect of his position on his character. Chicago was a rising and raw provincial metropolis. Hurstwood belonged in such a place. Such a man going to New York, where celebrities and rich *bons vivants* were so common, was practically doomed to failure. Consequently his passion for Carrie is not the sole reason for Hurstwood's undoing, for his tragic degradation. A man cannot escape from himself, from his own character. Hurstwood's tragedy begins when he abandons his social role in Chicago.

In general, the novel is based on a contrast between grandeur and misery. It also revolves around a further contrast: that of the rise of Carrie and the decline of Hurstwood. Unlike Hurstwood, Carrie is much less an individualized portrait. She is a social type, the "poor working girl" of the banal songs of the period, described realistically rather than sentimentally. What we see in Carrie is a pattern of American destiny. An aspiring girl with little intellect, who is all feeling and aspiration, she follows a typical course. Leaving the country—this was the period when the city was beginning to triumph decisively over the country—she is thrown helplessly into the turmoil of Chicago. She can advance, gain finery and luxury, do what she wants to do, give expression to her feelings only through a path of sin.

When the book was read by the publisher's wife, this pattern of destiny was shocking: it was revolting to the moral concepts of the era. And, withal, it was a social prediction. Today New York and Hollywood are full of Sister Carries: in fact, Sister Carrie is, in literature, a forecast of the type that has become the heroine of present-day gossip columns. She has become so familiar that one rarely even pauses to realize that Dreiser, more than forty years ago, revealed the genesis of this type, the motivations and the social factors that have perfected it.[3]

What is at the core in all of Dreiser's major works, including *Sister Carrie*, is the moral depth of the man's writings. Dreiser has always been concerned with the moral consequences implicit in the spectacle of wealth and poverty so apparent in our society. Evil is a problem to him, but he does not treat it in

---

[3] Carrie Muber, Eugene Witla, Frank Cowperwood, and Clyde Griffith are all young. In the case of Cowperwood, the man's career is described as being past youth, but it is to be observed that he becomes a great financial success while still young. It is interesting to note, in passing, the contrasts between these three characters. Carrie and Clyde both seek the same kind of end—success, advancement. It is suggestive that Carrie, a girl, succeeds, and that Clyde, in a later period, fails and is executed. This contrast in itself suggests the closing in of the chances of success, the increasing stratification of American life. Cowperwood is of an earlier period than Carrie. He violates the social codes, but succeeds—succeeds despite the fact that he is jailed. He is a realistically drawn young man of the period when opportunity was greatest in America. Further, the following contrast is interesting. The road to success for Cowperwood is business and finance, particularly the realm of finance which relates to speculation and manipulation. Carrie's avenue of success, like that of Eugene Witla, is art. For Clyde, the possibility of success is through family connections—rich relatives—and the opportunities they afford him of meeting rich people. Here is an illuminating contrast. It should suggest an additional reason as to why Mr. Dreiser's work is so important in American literature. In his probing effort to grasp forces socially operative in American society, he grasped the patterns of success, the patterns of social change, the way in which American patterns of destiny unfold in consonance with the operation of social forces and social laws.

theological terms. To him, evil is social: all his novels are concerned with the social history, the social processes of evil. Ambition, yearning, aspiration—these all revolve around this problem, and it in turn revolves around the role of money. He has related social causation—the basic social and economic factors that play a causal role in society—to individual patterns of destiny. His realism is a realism of social structures, and it was in *Sister Carrie* that he gave to American literature the first of his works of this character.

In essence, a book stands the test of time when we can translate its meaning into the experiences of our own time and see that it remains significant and alive. And that, I insist, can be done with *Sister Carrie*. It is one of the major novels in twentieth-century American literature.

1942

Ernest Hemingway's
The Sun Also Rises

ERNEST HEMINGWAY'S FIRST NOVEL, *The Sun Also Rises*, has been generally heralded as the definitive account of a war-wearied lost generation. In the light of this interpretation it is interesting to note that this novel was published in 1927, and that the time of its action is 1925. For these years fall within the most hopeful period of the post-Versailles world.

At that time there were many signs (at least in the eyes of superficial observers) to suggest that the world was returning to normalcy. After 1923, European capitalism seemed to have been restabilized, following the shocks of war, revolution, and dangers of revolution. At least to some, Germany looked like a going concern: the Weimar Republic was considered firmly secure. Hope was being revived in cartels as the means of achieving peaceable allocation of markets and equitable access to sources of raw materials. The epoch of disarmament talks, peace pacts, peace conferences had begun. America was in the full sweep of a tremendous economic boom, leading many to believe that this country was paving the way toward a new era of unprecedented world prosperity.

It may seem paradoxical that in such a period a novel of war disillusionment, nihilistic in outlook, should have become an international success.

However, this paradox is only superficial. With signs of a return to world prosperity there were growing evidences of pacifism. In particular, the youth which had been too young to have been in the trenches was deeply pacifistic. Disillusionment with the war was more or less accepted. In addition, a re-examination of the character of disillusionment portrayed in *The Sun Also Rises* suggests that this mood had become a way of feeling and acting; in fact, a social habit. By 1925 those who had been morally unhinged or physically maimed during the war had had a number of years in which to make some kind of adjustment to the postwar world. The period of the first difficult readjustment had passed. Such, for instance, is the case of the chief protagonist in *The Sun Also Rises*. Jake Barnes, impotent as a result of wounds suffered on the Italian front, has more or less reconciled himself to his condition.

Whenever there is a widespread mood of disillusionment caused by an event as catastrophic as a world war, that mood is bound to be nihilistic and rather adolescent in character unless it serves as the basis for a radical and progressive political orientation that aims to change and better the world. This is illustrated in *The Sun Also Rises*.

The characters express their bitterness, their feelings of disenchantment, with calculated bravado. Their conversation is reduced to enthusiastic small talk about their escapades. And this talk, as well as their actions, is largely a matter of pose and gesture. They act like people who have not fully grown up and who lack the self-awareness to realize this; in fact, they possess no desire to grow up.

The Sun Also Rises influenced younger persons more widely than it did members of Hemingway's own generation. He may have reflected the feelings of many who fought in the war; but most of these men were finding some way of settling down and adjusting themselves in the nineteen-twenties. Some were doing creative writing, some finding editorial jobs, some launching themselves in careers that later won them Pulitzer prizes in poetry and so on. This novel struck deeper chords in the youth of the Twenties.

Hemingway's first books had hardly been published when he had imitators all over America; furthermore, boys and girls on campus after campus began to talk like Hemingway characters. One need not go into detail to describe certain features of the Twenties; these are too fresh in our minds. Suffice it to say that by and large younger people were revolting against the standards and conventions of their elders, against the accepted notions of middle-class society. At the same time they were nonpolitical in their revolt. Add to this the deep pacifism of the decade, and one can easily understand why this novel struck such chords of response among young people, why Hemingway suddenly became the influence he did become at the time.

His influence was not merely superficial. It played a liberating and salutary role on those who would become the next generation of writers, and, more so, numerically, on readers. The hopes of those days have now been proved a snare by history. The nihilistic character of Hemingway's writing helped to free younger people from these false hopes. And although this novel (and many of his early stories as well) is set against a European background, Hemingway helped focus the eyes of younger people sharply on American life.

His writing was exciting and possessed of an extraordinary power of suggestiveness; it won over the reader to the feeling that he was actually participating in the lives of very real men and women. His use of dialogue helped enormously to create this impression. Others, notably Ring Lardner, preceded Hemingway in exploring and revealing the literary possibilities of the use of American vernacular, but he used it with amazing skill and originality. Both his suggestiveness in conveying a sense of life and his use of dialogue tended to turn the attention of youth toward common American experiences and to the speech expressing them on city streets and farms.

But Hemingway's influence, though so widespread, at the same time has been one that seems quickly to have exhausted itself. For Hemingway is a writer of limited vision, one who has no broad and fertile perspective on life. Younger writers were influenced—even seduced—by his moods; and they could grasp from him a sense of the great possibilities to be discovered in the true and simple treatment of common subject matter and in the use of ordinary speech. But once they had learned these lessons, they could gain little more from Hemingway.

The Europe described in *The Sun Also Rises* is a tourist's Europe of the Twenties. Cafés, restaurants, hotels, particularly of the Left Bank, are the setting. When the action shifts to Spain, it is to permit a magnificent description of bull fights and a fiesta. The mood and attitude of the main characters is that of people on a vacation. They set out to do what people want to do on a vacation: they have love affairs, they drink, go fishing, and see new spectacles. Written in the first person, the book unfolds from the standpoint of a spectator's attitude. Jake, the narrator, is a newspaper man; his is an occupation that naturally tends to develop the point of view of the spectator. Jake is constantly looking at the other characters, at himself, at the scenery of Spain, at the bull fight, at everything that occurs or comes within his view.

The main characters have only a meager past. They are escaping from their past and usually do not wish even to talk or to think of it. They live for the present, constantly searching for new and fresh sensations. They do not really think; even Jake scarcely thinks about himself or about his own impotence. These people feel quite alike. They form a small clique, stoically accepting the ills of their life.

Robert Cohn, however, is an outsider. He is with them because of his doglike love for Lady Brett Ashley. Unlike the others, he is unable to drown his feelings in banalities, small talk, and new spectacles. Cohn's difference from the others is one of the central points of the novel. This contrast is stated overtly when Lady Brett says that Cohn is "not one of us," and when Jake thinks that Cohn has behaved badly by pursuing Lady Brett. Focused against Cohn, Jake's simple, stoical attitude is enforced more strongly. The attitude of Jake is one of the basic attitudes in Hemingway's writings.

Hemingway's realism is, by and large, one which deals with sensations—with shocks to the senses. He has tended to reduce life to the effect that sights, scenes, and experiences make upon the nervous system; and he has avoided complicated types of response. Herein we find one of the major factors revealing his limitations as a writer.

In his most representative work he has saved himself from the crudities of simple behaviorism because of his gift of suggestiveness and his developed skill of understatement. The moral outlook in his work is on a plane of equal simplicity with his characters and subject matter. It amounts to the attitude that an action is good if it makes one feel good. Such an outlook on characters and events suggests that a development of greater understanding—broader range of feeling and sympathy, greater depth of imagination—is practically precluded.

This has been the case in Hemingway's career. He arrived on the literary scene absolute master of the style he has made his own; his attitudes were firmly fixed at that time. And he said pretty much what he had to say with his first stories and his first two novels.

As a novelist, it is my opinion that the best of Ernest Hemingway is still to be found in *The Sun Also Rises*. Its freshness has not faded with time. It remains one of the very best American novels of the Twenties.

1943

Mark Twain's Huckleberry Finn and Tom Sawyer

TO THE MEMORY OF FREDERICK ("POP") HENLE

MARK TWAIN has often been made the sport of critical fashions. During his lifetime he was slow in gaining recognition, except as a humorist. His writing, especially because of his views on the institution of monarchy, disturbed some of the literary democrats of the Eastern seaboard. His masterpiece, *The Adventures of Huckleberry Finn,* was barred from some public libraries. In general, too much of the critical writing on Mark Twain has stressed his failures and his limitations. His views on feudalism and, more generally, on thirteen centuries of Christian civilization have been misinterpreted, and he is sometimes pictured merely as the crass American frontiersman who could not rise to the level of appreciating the glories of European culture. It has been remarked that he might have corrected some of this gaucherié had he only known Henry Adams.[1]

While it is true that he was unhistorical in his approach to European culture, it nonetheless remains that many of his critics have been equally unhistorical. And, at the very least, there was in Twain a healthy sense of democratic feelings: a hatred of oppression and injustice, a deep-seated conviction that men were more important than the rags and cloth of the past, than

[1] Of the best known writers who misunderstand Mark Twain I would mention particularly Lewis Mumford (in *The Golden Day*) and Van Wyck Brooks. And it is surprising, to say the least, that Parrington lamented the fact that Twain did not know Henry Adams.

the trumpery, the show, the color, the glitter attached to out-
moded historic institutions. His attacks on romanticism were
literary necessities. In order to gain acceptance for what he
wanted to write, he had to attack the unhealthy influence that
this tradition exerted in America. As Bernard De Voto has
demonstrated in detail in *Mark Twain's America*, Twain's
source of inspiration was the frontier. He is the literary summation of pioneer America. And in *The Adventures of Huckleberry Finn*, he distilled and transmuted his material in terms
of great writing.

Mark Twain was both a genuine democrat and a cynic. As a
democrat he defended the Jacobins. Democratic ideas seemed
to be part of his very blood and flesh. His individualism, and
consequently his sense of the worth of human beings, is a direct product of democratic ideas. And he expressed these magnificently when he made an unschooled boy and a runaway
slave the heroes of what is truly an American odyssey. His
cynicism is related to the many disillusioning observations of
the failure of democratic ideas. In his most buoyant and productive periods, this cynicism is not sharply contradictory to
his democratic feelings. Rather, it suggests something of the
healthy cynicism of the *sansculottés*. In his latter days he witnessed the triumph of industrialism and the rapid expansion of
American capitalism. His conscience was disturbed, as were the
consciences of many writers and thinking people in both Europe and America. Then he became a bleak determinist somewhat on the order of the late Clarence Darrow. His cynicism
concerning "the damned human race" became corrosive. He
visioned the individual man alone in a dreary waste of empty
space. But his two boys, Tom and Huck, rise above his dis-
couragement, they are his strongest expression of democratic
hopes. Most particularly, Huck Finn is an ideal expression of
the positive side of Mark Twain.

It is significant that Tom and Huck are boys rather than
men, and therefore the more easily surrounded with an aura of
optimism. Whereas the adults in their Mississippi village look

down on Negro slaves as if they were not human beings, Tom
and Huck tend even to envy them. Less influenced by the village
standards, they can associate more freely with Negroes than can
adults. And consequently, Huck is able to come to grips with
the moral problems posed by the very existence of the institution of chattel slavery. Huck lives like a pioneer, like a squatter
in miniature. His respect for property rights is almost nil. To
filch watermelons and other food, to "borrow" someone else's
canoe, to ignore conventions and moral standards—none of this
troubles his conscience. But when it so happens that property
rights involve another human being, then he faces a moral
problem. This problem cuts into the heart of pre-Civil War
America. And Huck resolves the problem by deciding he will
have to help the Negro, Jim, even at the risk of eternal damnation. To help a Negro slave escape is a "low-down thing to do."
A person "don't want to take no consequence of it." The more
this problem troubles Huck, "the more my conscience kept
grinding me, and the more wicked and low-down and ornery
I got to feeling." He tries to soften his conscience by convincing himself that he was brought up "wicked." He tries to pray,
"but one can't pray a lie." He plans to write Jim's owner a
letter and thereby save himself from this evil. He can't. The
humanity of Jim outweighs the moral code of Huck's environment. Huck makes a moral choice: he helps Jim to escape.
He is in it for good, so he will go "the whole hog." Here we see
Huck affirming the value of a living human being of the present as against the claims justified in an institution of the past.
And this affirmation is the very core of Mark Twain's own
sense of the worth of human beings. To continue: Tom and
Huck are shrewd, daring, ingenious. These are traits that Mark
Twain admired. Tom Sawyer is the type of boy who could
grow up to be a Pudd'nhead Wilson. The resourcefulness of
Huck parallels that of the Connecticut Yankee. Thus, when
Tom and Huck outwit adults, we must not interpret these
passages merely as humor. Through his two unspoiled boys
Twain forcefully emphasized his own attitudes and values.

The Adventures of Tom Sawyer is a boy's book. Its sequel,

The Adventures of Huckleberry Finn, is an adult's novel. However, the two books should not be considered separately, for Tom and Huck are contrasts. Tom is a romantic; Huck, a realist. At first this temperamental difference seems paradoxical when we think of the circumstances of their lives. Tom lives a regular life. Cared for by his Aunt Polly, he is an accepted member of the community. He is sent to school, is taken to church and Sunday school, and he goes on picnics with other children whose parents also live orderly lives. He becomes the boyhood sweetheart of Becky Thatcher, whose father is one of the leading figures in the village. Tom seeks to escape from regularity by romanticism. He feeds on detective and adventure stories (in fact, the very characterization of Tom constitutes a satire on this form of writing), and he strives to translate what he reads into the real world around him. Huck, on the contrary, is a realist living under romantic circumstances. There is no order in his life. He is a child of whim and impulse, heedless of authority and convention. The other boys are warned by their parents and their teacher not to associate with him. But Huck represents common sense as opposed to romanticism. Since his problems are of a life-and-death character, he must be a realist in order to survive. Tom's real problems are settled for him, so that he is more concerned with those of his imagination. Huck, equally adventurous, cannot afford the luxury of romanticism.

As a result of these differences, Huck appears to be more mature than Tom, although they are of the same age. At the conclusion of *The Adventures of Huckleberry Finn,* Tom seems to be the same charming boy he was when we first met him, while Huck has developed and grown in character, having acquired a clearer and purer sense of moral values. It is this fact that explains the difference between the two books—revealed also in the humor, which is much more pointed in the second novel. There was usually a devastating attack behind the playfulness and humor of Mark Twain. The extravaganza, the burlesque included in the saga of Huck Finn is pointed at the old South and cuts to the heart of a whole society. The sharpest humor in *The Adventures of Tom Sawyer* strikes less deeply; it is directed at adventure writing and at the school system of the period. But, taken together, both boys stand in contrast to "the damned human race."

The institution of chattel slavery always forms the background against which these boys live. It forces itself into the very content of consciousness, not only of Tom and Huck, but of all the members of their village. As Bernard De Voto has pointed out, the existence of slavery explains the role that superstition plays in the minds of Tom and Huck. Here Mark Twain made a neat social comment. He told us, in effect, that if we preserve the institution of slavery it will permeate our entire culture and become a formidable barrier to progress. Just as slavery produces meanness and brutality, so does it perpetuate magic. Briefly, the backwardness of the slaves, treated as property rather than as human beings, will blunt the moral and intellectual development of the masters. Twain's penetrating revelation of the moral and social consequences of slavery is focused in the relationship between Huck and Jim, the runaway slave, for it is through intimate association with him that Huck's moral landscape is broadened. Huck must even learn that a Negro can love his family as tenderly as white folks do. Jim shines through the novel as a man with dignity, loyalty, and courage. Drifting along the Mississippi, he assumes heroic proportions, demonstrating by contrast that many of the white men surrounding him are cruel or foolish. This is most clearly drawn in the case of the King and the Duke, who are rascals, but who are also symbolic figures, representing the dead institutions of the past. And Huck makes the symbolism explicit when he tells Jim that they are not at all bad when one considers what real kings and dukes have done in history.

It need not be stressed that Mark Twain re-created almost a full sense of life on the Mississippi. This is undisputed. He wrote with ease and buoyancy: there is humor, sensibility, and beauty in his style. But there is real penetration, too. He evokes an entire epoch, by giving it form, solidity, depth.

Generations of Americans have read of these two boys. They

have become part of the consciousness of most literate people
in this country, and one feels, on rereading their stories, as if
one is meeting old and imperishable friends. But they do not
represent merely the idyllic times of boyhood. The world in
which they lived was full of its own cruelties. One reason they
are so charming is that we see their unspoiled images flashed
against the mirror of that world. Tom and Huck are symbols
of the possibilities in human beings. Today they stand as a test
not only of ourselves but of the whole of American society.
They are, with all their charm, like two accusing figures, with
their fingers pointing down the decades of American history.
Their very characters seem to ask why—why has this promise
not been realized? Why is it so rarely that the man becomes
what the boy gave promise of becoming? This is part of
their significance as enduring characters in American literature.

Ring Lardner's Round Up

RING LARDNER began his career in fiction most unpretentiously with *You Know Me Al* and other baseball stories. These pieces are lighter, gayer than his later work. He took the heroes of the sports pages and showed that they were made of anything but the cloth of heroism. Some of them were eccentric Yahoos; others were boasting braggarts, irascible and childish in their vanity. Later he scored the same points with greater melancholy, with increased scorn. His most important work is contained in the collection of his stories, *Round Up;* this book has attained both a wide popular audience and a high critical praise. It is well worth discussing now, more than a decade after Lardner's death.

The first trait that strikes you about most of Lardner's characters is their intense competitiveness. When they are not engaging in some highly competitive business or sport, they are amusing themselves with a cutthroat game of bridge or golf. And they exhibit this same intensity in their social climbing and in the contempt they feel for anyone not exactly like themselves. Almost all of them have the same social standards: they are busy not only keeping up with, but getting ahead of, the Joneses—with the Joneses, that is, whose names appear on the society pages.

They are so competitive, in fact, that they can scarcely play a game of solitaire, or even a solitary round of golf, without cheating themselves. Their bragging is generally calculated to

31

prove how clever they are—how good at checkers, prize-fighting, baseball, golf, or bridge; how well traveled they are; how many rich people they have met; how well they dance—in short, with how much envy the world should regard them.

We really see, however, that these people do not fit the images they present to the world. For one thing, they are among the most banal characters in all modern American fiction; in fact, I doubt if any other American writer of this century has so skillfully and so extensively used banality as did Ring Lardner. Besides being banal, these characters are ignorant, too, but this is not their major deficiency; if it were, the spectacle they present would be less depressing. Chiefly, they are bores: they interrupt card games, conversations, amusements, in order to indulge their seemingly endless interest in themselves. But even their love of monologues is not the fundamental quality about them. Rather it is their moral code—if such it may be described.

In general, whenever a Lardner character performs an act of kindness, is sympathetic or generous to someone else, he or she is taken advantage of; in this world the decent person is a sucker. Likewise, if any of these characters dares give vent to a genuine feeling—a feeling that is delicate, expressive, unsmothered in the dreary and sometimes vicious sentimentality which passes for feeling in this world—he is regarded as a comic.

Here is a world in which the principle of *caveat emptor* applies recurrently in social relationships, in human relationships of love, friendship or family. Thus the satire of Ring Lardner reveals the working out of the mechanisms of American civilization. By depicting, in terms of social life, an extension of the competitive system, Lardner reveals certain consequences of the rise of American economy and American civilization. He tells us what many comfortable, successful, and even rich and famous people are like as human beings—documenting the terrible or dreary cost of success in terms of what happens to the human personality.

Lardner's characters are the "rugged individualists" of the

baseball diamond, the prize ring, Broadway, the golf links, the card table or the Pullman car; the terrible irony emerging from his stories is that here they are these rugged individualists, doing what they claim they want to do—enjoying the fruits of money, fame, prestige, buying the comforts available to American wealth—here they are, alike as rubber stamps. Their main desire is to be a better rubber stamp than the next person. And they are so proud of themselves! They expect to be liked, admired, envied, because they are precisely what they are. As is usually the case in satire, vices are paraded for virtues; here social vices strut, eager for praise and applause.

The meaning of Ring Lardner's stories can, I believe, be made more concrete if we contrast two of them—"A Caddy's Diary" and "Golden Honeymoon." In the first of these we meet the youngest character of *Round Up*, a sixteen-year-old caddy at a golf club, the members of which are the best (that is, the richest) people of a characteristic small town. The boy keeps a diary, hoping that he will thereby learn to write, and make money as a writer. He has also acquired the ambition to make an easy living as a golf pro.

The prosperous golfers at the club are all pretty much the same. They all have the same passion to win and to appear better players than they are. The boy becomes popular—earning big tips—by catering to their vanities and by helping them conceal their real scores. The pretty lady whom he admires is no different from the rest; she allows him to cheat for her so that, in competition with another woman, she may win a dress she doesn't need. The richest man in town does likewise, in order to win a prize of nine golf balls instead of six. One of the club members becomes unpopular when he absconds with eight thousand dollars of his bank's money. But the caddy wonders if it is any sillier to cheat for eight thousand dollars than for a dress or three golf balls. He concludes—establishing one of Lardner's major points—that "these people have got a lot of nerve to pan Mr. Crane" (the absconder) "and call him a sucker for doing what he done, it seems to me like eight thousand dollars

. . . is a pretty fair reward compared with what some of these people sell their soul for, and I would like to tell them about it."

The caddy speaks for Ring Lardner. In his days as a working sports writer and newspaper humorist he saw people doing just these things. He told of it with barbed humor, with gaiety, and later with the most mordant irony of any writer of his generation. This story also establishes the meanings of the Lardner world in another sense, for it shows the ideals and habits of this world operationally: its standards influencing the younger generation, pointing out to youth a way to success and ease.

The caddy has a sincerity that most of Lardner's adults lack —otherwise he would never have posed the moral question he did—but he is destined to lose that sincerity and become like the adults. Thus, we can interpret this story as describing more or less how a Lardner character gets that way.

Contrasted with this boy are the old couple of "Golden Honeymoon." This story stands at the other boundary of the Ring Lardner world, so to speak, revealing what has happened to the oldest protagonist of *Round Up*. After fifty-two years of marriage, the old man describes, in monologue, the couple's golden honeymoon trip to Florida. This is a very funny story. And yet, under its affectionate humor, we are troubled by a sense of emptiness and futility. Lardner's ear for speech has recorded accurately the sound of an old man reciting time tables, telling us when the trains arrived at and departed from a succession of railroad stations on the way to Florida. We see an old man so drained of inner life, of feelings, of curiosity, that the time table itself has become highly meaningful.

In Florida we learn, as if we were listening to the recitation of more time tables, that the couple stayed in a rooming house and how they met the man who had years ago been a rival for "Mother's" hand. Flashes of a jealousy, dead for fifty-two years, occur as the two old men play checkers, horseshoes, "five hundred," and vie as to the cafeterias at which they eat and the excellence of the States in which they live. The narrator feels that he is the better man when he wins at checkers, and offers involved explanations as to why he lost at cards and horse-shoes. His petulance finally breaks up the foursome and ends the amusements which were all the two old couples had in common.

The story ends with a recitation of time tables on the return trip. What underscores the impression of emptiness is that now it makes no difference who was the better man in the rivalry for Mother's hand. The winner and the loser are no different from each other; had their roles been reversed fifty-two years ago, they would still be the same as we see them in their old age. "The Golden Honeymoon" thus closes the cycle of experience whose beginning was described in "A Caddy's Diary."

Others have written satire with more pretension, or with a greater surface scope; but to my mind no other American writer has achieved Lardner's mastery of satire. His knife was sharper; it cut more deeply—so deeply, in fact, that these people who seem so dreary, so banal, so self-centered, often emerge for us as yearning, unhappy creatures who are lost, deprived and vaguely unsatisfied.

There is a singular contradiction in nearly all these people. Living an intense social life, they are antisocial. They can never really establish human relationships with one another. Seemingly always together, they are alone, unable to reach across a world bounded by their own skins. They are continually talking to establish a public image of themselves, as if they were filled with some ungratified yearning, some hole in their spirits which must forever be a vacuum. They are singularly repressed. They do not know how to be friends, they do not know how to love one another. Their loves are framed in the language of the popular songs, and as quickly die. Often, underneath the sentimental image of love, a cancer exists, as in "The Love Nest." Bored with themselves, they bore one another, and then, with renewed energy, with restored lung power, they plunge forth again into another dreary card game, another dull vacation, another empty, even pitiful, little escapade.

Now and then there escapes from one of these people a cry of frustration, a cry which at least verges on agony and loneliness. Such is the last letter of the girl in one of the most masterful of these stories, "Some Like Them Cold." Her correspondent has bragged, encouraged her, led her on, and then tells her coldly that he is to marry another girl. She is deeply hurt; the image of herself she tried to create in his mind has not been accepted; and she writes: "I have something better to do than read letters from a man like you, specially as I have a man friend who is not so generous as Miss Sears [his fiancée] and would strongly object to my continuing a correspondence with another man."

She ends with a nasty dig at the fiancée, asking how a girl can have a good time married to a man who makes only sixty dollars a week. We know that she is probably destined to go through the same disappointment again, that she is lonely and frustrated, that she cannot admit a defeat which has so hurt her. We know that her disappointment will leave a lasting scar of bitterness.

Here we see the significance of these characters trying to create fantastic public images of themselves. Here is the pathos of emptiness. And it is this pathos which deepens the stories of Ring Lardner, which gives a melancholy overtone of humanity to his cold and objective portraits of all these dullards, these child egomaniacs, these trivial "regular fellows." This is the essence of his writing—writing which has won for itself an enduring place in contemporary American fiction.

1944

Dostoievsky's
The Brothers Karamazov

The Brothers Karamazov is the last novel Dostoievsky wrote. In it he wanted to express—"at least once" before he died—all that he felt and believed. It is the summation of a lifetime of tormented creative activity.

Dostoievsky conceived character as the product of belief. In his work a man is principally that which he believes. And *The Brothers Karamazov* is Dostoievsky's broadest, his most general study of problems of belief. It is a dramatic and psychological representation of the moral consequences involved in the acceptance or rejection of the existence of God. If atheism be accepted, then what basis is there for moral action? Without God, man, the individual man himself, is the ultimate arbiter of what is good and bad. And if this be so, why does not anything go, even, let us say, Raskolnikov's murder in *Crime and Punishment*? Here Dostoievsky was attacking Western bourgeois ethics, which are based on ideas of self-interest and self-development. Behind them he saw the specters of atheism and revolution, and Holy Russia must be saved from these. Failing to see the progressive aspects of the historical development of the ideas of individualism, Dostoievsky extended these ideas to one logical extreme, which focused them as an ethic of the jungle. He dramatized these problems and conceptions by constructing his novel around the contrasting personalities and beliefs of two of the Karamazov brothers, Ivan and Alyosha.

The former is a doubter, a Russian Hamlet type, influenced by Western ideas, who seeks to order his life on the basis of rationalism. He fails, and because of his doubts drives himself into brain fevers which threaten his life. Alyosha, a man of faith, tries to approximate the example of Christ. Unlike his brothers, he is integrated, optimistic, adjusted to his environment. Thus he serves as a symbol of the author's own faith and becomes, as a result, the ideal Dostoievskian character.

In 1854 Dostoievsky wrote in a personal letter:

"I . . . am a child of this age . . . of unfaith and skepticism, and probably . . . shall remain so to the end of my life. How dreadfully it has tormented me . . . this longing for faith. . . . God sometimes gives me moments of perfect peace; in such moments I love and believe that I am loved; in such moments I have formulated my creed, wherein all is clear and holy to me. This creed is extremely simple . . . I believe that there is nothing lovelier, deeper, more sympathetic, more rational, more manly than the Saviour; I say to myself with jealous love that not only is there no one else like Him, but that there could be no one. I would even say more: If anyone could prove to me that Christ is outside the truth, and if the truth did exclude Christ, I should prefer to stay with Christ and not with truth."

For him, belief was a psychological necessity. The writings of the sick and tortured man of genius are, on the whole, permeated with an intense and passionate determination to attain belief and to be well, to be normal and psychologically healthy. In literature he struggled to attain self-integration, inner harmony. The three Karamazov brothers are, in one sense, an objectification of his own consciousness. Ivan represents the doubting side of his nature; Mitya objectifies his own volatile personality, with its sharp changes from fevered and reckless gambling to moods of remorse, and then to sudden flights of lofty aspiration. And Alyosha idealizes what he wanted to be. In creating Alyosha he attained a sense of that inner harmony which he was never to gain in his personal life. *The Brothers Karamazov* is remarkable in its revelation of the author's intense effort to attain self-integration.

These three characters symbolize not only Dostoievsky but Russia herself. Thus Mitya is Russia as he conceived her to be, capable of great deeds and equally capable of great shame. Ivan is a symbolic prediction of the dire catastrophe awaiting Russia if she should succumb to Western ideas and thereby reject her Russian God, her Russian Church, her Czar, and her historic Russian destiny. This interpretation of the novel reveals how Dostoievsky twined his Slavophilism into the very warp and woof of his story. Toward the end of this novel we see Alyosha with the schoolboys who gather at the bedside of the dying Illusha. Alyosha influences these boys, particularly their leader Kolya, who can become either an Alyosha or an Ivan. And after Alyosha addresses them, following the burial of Illusha, they cheer: "Hurrah for Karamazov!" This, the last line of the novel, is both a political affirmation and an implicit appeal to the youth of Russia to reject Western ideas and the revolution.[1]

In order to establish these affirmations, Dostoievsky presents an image of man which, again, is principally symbolized in the three brothers. Mitya is representative of the body; Ivan is symbolic of the mind; Alyosha typifies the spirit. If man merely satisfies the needs and impulses of the body, he is a slave of his own passions. He is a sensualist, like Mitya and the elder Karamazov. He is a prisoner of himself, and he sins. But Dostoievsky regarded sin as being naive and childish rather than evil. In his eyes the sinner was a compassionate figure. Man punishes himself for his sins by his own shame and by his self-imposed moral torments. And if man rises from the plane of the body to that of the mind, he is still not free. Then he becomes the victim of doubt and skepticism, and to Dostoievsky skepticism was evil, diabolical. Ivan, one of the most brilliant young men in all nineteenth-century literature, is a pure rationalist. He grapples with problems of faith and belief because he wants to order his

[1] In a letter to some students written in 1878, also, Dostoievsky urged them to go and remain with the people and to "believe in God which is impossible for Russian Europeans . . ."

life on the basis of pure reason. His end is disastrous. Man gains freedom only by transcending both the body and the mind and by living in the spirit. The life of the spirit is one of faith, of love, and of suffering. The ideal of human freedom is the suffering Christ who died on the cross in order to redeem the sins of all mankind. To be free one must follow the example of Christ.

The real hero of this novel is Christ, the Dostoievskian Christ. In the framework of the novel there is a succession of influences which establish this ideal and reveal it in operation. Alyosha's teacher, Father Zossima, presents the case for God against atheism. He teaches the doctrines of the Dostoievskian Christ. He influences Alyosha, who, in turn, serves as an example for the schoolboys.

Dostoievsky's image of Christ is that of a man more human than other men.[2] He is God because he is the most human, the most compassionate, the most suffering of all men. Thus the question of miracles is important. Dostoievsky takes great pains to demonstrate that there are no miracles in the supernatural sense of the word. When Father Zossima dies and a miracle is expected, Dostoievsky describes how the corpse of the Elder decays with unusual rapidity. The mortal flesh of the Elder, propagator of Christ on earth, is even more corruptible than is most flesh. And Father Zossima's rival, Father Ferrapont, is an unbalanced hermit who believes in miracles and who is forever exorcising devils. This contrast is important. It emphasizes what Dostoievsky regarded as the real miracle in life— Christlike love, which alone can save humanity.

Dostoievsky, a Christian, a Slavophile, a defender of Czarism, did not merely seek to preserve values as they were. He tried to forge new values for Christianity. While his beliefs and ideas were traditional, his psychology was revolutionary. He was a man of the nineteenth century, profoundly influenced by the current of ideas that he opposed with such bitter intensity. As a psychologist, he anticipated Freud. In an operational sense, he introduced the unconscious mind in fiction.

2 This should make it clear that in Dostoievsky, there are definite elements similar to Protestantism.

This explains the element of compulsion, of obsession, in his writing about the nineteenth-century European. And we find that it anticipates our own century. The popularity of Dostoievsky in our own time is to be explained largely on the basis of this aspect of his writing. For instance, the comments of Father Zossima are those of a nineteenth-century man rather than of a traditional Christian. Dostoievsky's real greatness is expressed in his revolutionary psychological insight. Although he himself believed in the Russian soul, that which he presented as the Russian soul is more correctly described as the human soul struggling with problems poignantly felt in the nineteenth century.

Dostoievsky was a novelist of the consciousness of man. His work is an objectification of the human consciousness presented on the plane of action. This explains the extremism of his characters and the melodrama of his plots. He turned his characters inside out, and their actions are objectifications of their inner life. This is one of the means by which he revealed character as the product of belief. His dialogue is singularly frank. His characters do not hesitate to pour out their inmost shames, thoughts, aspirations, self-abasements, in frenzied streams of conversation which will often run through more than one long chapter. His use of dialogue is a device, one which serves the same purpose as does the interior monologue of the modern novel.

It is also to be noted that in Dostoievsky's work there are fewer descriptions of objects and of the objective world than is the case, say, in the writings of his contemporaries Turgenev and Tolstoy. His characters often walk down streets and see almost nothing of the external world; at times they don't even know where they are walking and find they have taken a certain course because of some unknown inner compulsion. His proud women are amazingly lacking in a sense of their own physical attributes; they show little interest in their own adornment, or in the arrangement of furniture, or of objects and colors in their own household. Like the male characters, they, too, are concerned with their inner consciousness. And when money plays a role in one of his plots, as it does in the case of Mitya, it is more significant as a symbol connected with pride than as a medium of exchange.

With such an orientation, it is understandable that Dostoievsky's conception of inevitability is psychological. As such it is to be distinguished from the inevitability embodied in naturalistic novels; a product of socially determined conditions and laws that prevent man from enforcing his decisions in the outer world. In Dostoievsky, inevitability is expressed as moral torment. The punishment for a crime in his world is self-imposed moral torment which precedes any punishment inflicted by society; in fact, the latter is the stage for a man's regeneration. Writing from such perspectives, and using such means as these, he was able to cut under the conventional conceptions of what is normal and what is abnormal, and thereby attained a deeper and more profound sense of what man is like.

Dostoievsky reflected Russia standing between the old and the new, between the past and the future. He posed the same essential problem that Tolstoy did in *Anna Karenina,* although in terms of morals and beliefs. Basically, it was a question of what should be done, and Dostoievsky's answer was to affirm the Russian past. He threw the whole weight of his genius into an effort to stop the clock of history. Although this novel is one of faith and affirmation, it is one of the most deeply pessimistic novels of the nineteenth century. It offered to mankind only a perspective of endless suffering, as if the purgatory excluded from the doctrines of the Orthodox Church were transferred to this earth. He was convinced that Western methods to alleviate suffering by conquering nature would never make man happier; that the revolution would only produce catastrophe; that man must suffer; that the noblest man is he who suffers not only for himself but for all his fellowmen. He believed that since the world cannot be changed, man must be changed by love.

Modern history is warrant enough to indicate that mankind

does not, and will not, accept such a fatalistic perspective. Russia did not accept it from Dostoievsky. That which he fought triumphed; that which he affirmed, had no future, even in his own lifetime. Regardless of what one thinks of the Russian revolution, it should be clear by now that in Czarist Russia there was no other force that could offer hope of regeneration and liberation. Backward Russia was moving forward to enter modern history in the full sense of the meaning of these words. And this is what Dostoievsky fought with all the intensity and passion of his genius. But he could not regenerate that which history had already sentenced as doomed. His appeal to the youth of Russia ultimately fell on deaf ears.

Today certain basic values remain in his writings, which should persist as moral values in any future form of society. He wrote with candor, honesty, penetration, and high seriousness. He came to grips with problems the importance of which we all must recognize. His novels are marked by a penetrating insight that has rarely been equaled in literature. His work is pervaded with profound compassion. If it is true, as Chekhov declared, that if one would make man better, one must make him see what he is, then we can readily recognize the lasting value of Dostoievsky.

For in his tormented struggles to write he was constantly striving to gain a clearer, a more fundamental image of what men and women were like. He hid nothing of consequence in his novels. He truly re-created the grandeur and the misery of human consciousness. One of his major achievements was that of conveying to future ages a profound sense of the worth of individual human beings. Almost ironically, his work contains an emphasis on the worth of a human being similar to that found in the work of Western writers who forged the ideas of individualism.

The tides of history have engulfed Dostoievsky's hopes but not his fame nor the importance of his contributions. These are living influences. His works, especially *The Brothers Karamazov* and *Crime and Punishment*, are endless sources of insight and inspiration to writers and to readers of many lands. His genius triumphed where his ideas failed. His own life was tormented, tragic, even terrible. But at its very end he did achieve his aim of expressing all that he felt and believed—"at least once" —before he died. And that expression forms one of the greatest masterpieces in world literature.

1943

Joyce's A Portrait of the Artist as a Young Man[1]

I

"THIS RACE and this country and this life produced me," declares Stephen Dedalus—artistic image of James Joyce himself —in *A Portrait of the Artist as a Young Man*. The *Portrait* is the story of how Stephen was produced, how he rejected that which produced him, how he discovered that his destiny was to become a lonely one of artistic creation. It is well to look into this life out of which Stephen came, to discuss the social and national background of this novel. In Ireland a major premise of any discussion of her culture and of her literature is an understanding of Irish nationalism. And it is at least arguable that Joyce was a kind of inverted nationalist. The nationalism he rejects runs through him like a central thread.

Ireland, when James Joyce was a boy, suffered from a profound political defeat, the fall of Parnell. In that, once again, she was set back in her long struggle to attain nationhood. The aftermath was marked by a deeply felt and pervasive bitterness, often expressed in feelings of personal betrayal. And the *Portrait* reflects these moods. The brilliantly written scene, early in the novel, of the Dedalus family pitilessly quarreling at the Christ-

[1] When this article was written the earlier version of Joyce's novel, titled *Stephen Hero*, was not available to me. The article, therefore, was written with no knowledge of this work other than that gathered from writings about it that seemed to me basically uninformative. I have since read *Stephen Hero*, but it does not cause me to change this analysis.

mas dinner table is a highly concentrated artistic representation
of the magnitude of Parnell's fall in Ireland, of how it cut
through families with a knifelike sharpness. The family argument is personal and its passionate anger seems to be in inverse
proportion to the political impotence of those who are hurling
insults at one another.

Whenever Stephen, as a youth, discusses politics, he expresses
himself with resentment. He identifies himself with the coura-
geous men who have striven for, and been martyred in, the cause
of Ireland, feeling that they have been let down by their own
followers, by those whom they were trying to free. Stephen's
reaction is not a singular one for the Ireland of his time.
(In fact, it is even paralleled in this period, for just as Stephen
blames the Irish people for Ireland's defeats, so do many contemporary radical intellectuals blame the workers for the defeats of socialism.) The Irish people have betrayed the future
of Stephen Dedalus. This is the real sense of his bitterness. Even
the monuments and memorials to Ireland's honorable heroes,
Tone and Emmet, are tawdry, part of a tawdry Dublin present
which he resents.

Ireland's national aspirations generalized real, deep-seated
needs. These had been choked up in the nineteenth century by
a whole series of defeats, from the time of Emmet and Tone to
that of Parnell. When such wide needs are thus thwarted, frustrated, they are revealed in a molecular way, a sense of multiple
personal betrayal, despair and disgust with politics. And when
such a social phenomenon is expressed in art, it usually is in
terms of how it is immediately felt rather than in terms of its
social rationale. This is how Stephen felt about the Irish political
defeats, directly, and with painful immediacy.

The post-Parnell period was one of groping for new orientation. Irish nationalism found this politically in Sinn Fein and
culturally in the so-called Irish Literary Renaissance, the Gaelic-
language movement, and the Gaelic-sports movement.

In a diary note (quoted in Herbert Gorman's valuably in-
formative biography) Joyce once described Ireland as "an after-
thought of Europe." This remark is to be interpreted as relat-

ing principally to Ireland's cultural backwardness. During the nineteenth century, Ireland, a backward country, suffering from continuous economic crises, lived through a succession of miseries. Famine, emigration, defeat—this was her lot. Irish culture was meager; it was also debased by much that was counterfeit, for instance, the literature of the stage Irishman. What culture there was had been nourished by the liberating influences of the great French Revolution and found its best expression in such patriots as Thomas Davis and James Clarence Mangan, as well as in the novelist William Carleton. Ireland's experiences gave her thin culture a tincture of sadness, at times a romantic sadness; an instance of this is Mangan's "Dark Rosaleen." In the first half of the nineteenth century a disunified Germany created a German philosophy which, with Hegel, achieved a kind of spiritual unity in culture as a sublimation of the real need for the unity which was not attained on the plane of history. When there was a sudden growth of this thin Irish culture in the post-Parnell period, it can be explained as a similar kind of cultural compensation.

There is a note of foreignness, of alienness, in the first stage of the Irish literary renaissance. Nationalists often call it an Anglicized culture; what I think they really mean is that it did not adequately express Irish needs of the time. The progenitors of this movement were very talented people, and one of them, Yeats, was destined to become probably the greatest poet of his age writing in the English language. But they went to Irish materials as if from without. Sensitive to a disorientation that was pervasively felt at the time, needing sources of inspiration fresher than those of English literature and of the *fin de siècle* when Victorian culture fell apart, they more or less discovered Ireland.

But what did they discover? This stage of the so-called renaissance produced the poetic drama. It found thematic material in the legends of Ireland's free and pre-Saxonized past. A fresh and poetic language was sought in the speech of the poorest, the most backward section of Irish peasantry. Standish O'Grady, frequently referred to as the father of this movement, attempted to re-establish the old legends on a Homeric level. It seems as if all these writers were seeking to create images of great figures of their past in order to compensate (though perhaps not consciously) for their lack of leaders in the present; so that, with Parnell gone, they could still derive some cultural subsistence, some sense of pride and inspiration, from the image of Fergus and other heroes of the legends.[2] Thwarted on the historical plane, Ireland set up as a counter to England an idea of her own culture. Through culture, she would show that she was a nation. When Yeats wrote a play like *Kathleen ni Houlihan* with political implications, it is interesting to note that Kathleen ni Houlihan (Ireland, and a rather weak cultural image to set against that of John Bull) asks her sons not to live, fight, win, and build for her, but rather to go and die for her, as if Ireland had been lacking in names to inscribe on her martyrology.

The emphasis of this stage of the movement was on the past. Where could Joyce fit into it? What could it teach him, a young genius who was so acutely sensitive to all the life of the moment? In the *Portrait*, the world presses on Stephen. His own thoughts are melancholy. His proud spirit cannot tolerate the painful burden of reality. He must rise above it. All this burden is not directly represented in the novel; some of it is reflected in memory and in conversation. No clear and full picture of Stephen's relationship with his mother is described. Through

[2] Generally speaking, national cultural movements tend to create a sense of pride in a nation, in a national culture. There can be no doubt but that this is involved in the Irish cultural renaissance. However, it had other aspects also. For Ireland it has its clear-cut romantic emphasis. There is, therefore, something of romantic substitution to be seen in this movement. The idea of the nation, and of a national Irish culture is clearer, more political, a more conscious idea in the minds of earlier Irish writers—that is, Thomas Davis and John Mitchell. Listen to D. J. O'Donoghue, editor of Davis's essays, on Davis: "In a few words he sought to impress upon Irishmen the fact that they had much to be proud of in their history and their character, and he saw that the surest way to induce a nation to rise to higher things was to imbue them with the idea that they had already accomplished much." And John Mitchell said of Davis that the latter wrote "from a calm, deliberate conviction that among other agencies for arousing national spirit, fresh, manly, vigorous national songs and ballads must by no means be neglected . . ." There is clearly a difference in the ideas of cultural nationalism in the case of Davis and Mitchell, on one hand, and in the Yeats of *Kathleen ni Houlihan* on the other.

conversation, we learn that he has had a distressing quarrel with her, in which he tells her that he has lost his faith. In addition, Stephen loses his respect for his father; he begins to develop that feeling of being fatherless which is so important a part of his character in *Ulysses*. But here Joyce does not develop these relationships in directly written scenes. Much is not touched upon—for instance, what of the relationship between Stephen's father and mother?

The *Portrait* contains only a most highly concentrated sense of home, school, streets, and city which press so sharply upon Stephen's spirit. He is acutely sensitive to all that happens around him: he breathes in something of every wind which blows in Ireland. Joyce at this time felt more, saw more, brooded more than he allows Stephen to reveal to us. Stephen, as boy and youth, tramps the streets of Dublin. Sometimes in his walks he trembles with fears of damnation. Again, his mind is filled with lurid visions of sin, written of in purple passages suggestive of Pater's prose; but very often he searches, looks, listens. In these walks how much of Dublin must have attracted him, how much must have repelled him! How much didn't the streets of Dublin tell him of life, of men, of himself? How much of Ireland's real, historic past was not poured through his senses, into the pulsing life of the present? Why is Stephen so melancholy? Obviously because he carries within him such a burden of impressions, such a burden of the life of his country, his city, his race, his own family.

What Stephen sees is Irish history in the present, in terms of what has happened to Ireland and to Irishmen as a result of her defeats. But Stephen does not dwell on a tragic past in moods of regret. Rather, he is bitter because of the condition of the Ireland he knows, the Ireland inherited from a tragic historic past. During the period when he was still at work on *A Portrait of the Artist as a Young Man*, Joyce, in a letter, describes Dublin as a "center of paralysis." It should be realized that it was Joyce who introduced the city realistically into modern Irish writing. The city—Dublin—is the focus of Ireland in his work, and in his life. We see that this is the case with Stephen, the genius son of a declassed family. Stephen lives, grows up in a Dublin that is a center of paralysis. Is he to have a future in such a center? Is he to prevent himself from suffering paralysis, spiritual paralysis? Stephen's painful burden of reality can be interpreted as a reality that derives from the history of Ireland's defeats and that is focused, concretized, in the very quality of the men of Dublin. Stephen describes his own father to a friend as "A medical student, an oarsman, a tenor, an amateur actor, a shouting politician, a small landlord, a small investor, a drinker, a good fellow, a storyteller, somebody's secretary, something in a distillery, a tax gatherer, a bankrupt, and at present a praiser of his own past." Just as Stephen says he has been produced by "This race and this country and this life," so can this be said of his father. It is in this way, and in the image of his own father, that we can realize how Stephen carries a sense of Ireland's history in his own consciousness. And at the same time he feels that he is a foreigner in Dublin, a foreigner in the sense that he is even forced to speak a language not his own. Just before his discussion of esthetics with the Jesuit dean of studies, Stephen realizes that "The Ireland of Tone and of Parnell seemed to have receded in space." He, Stephen, living in the Ireland after their failure, thinks, while talking to the dean: "I cannot speak or write these words without unrest of spirit. His language [the dean's], so familiar and so foreign, will always be for me an acquired speech. I have not made or accepted its words. My voice holds them at bay. My soul frets in the shadow of his language." Stephen's thoughts are highly suggestive, highly important, for an interpretation of this novel. When Joyce walked the streets of Dublin as a youth, one can be sure he constantly sensed the presence of the English in the major city of Ireland. One can speculate by asking how many little incidents, words, gestures, angers, glances of suspicion did he not grasp on the wing, all deepening a sense of the life of Dublin as a painful burden? The failure of the Irish to follow men like Tone and Parnell, meant that he, Stephen, must fret in speaking a language not his own. Again, it is revealed how Irish history presses on Stephen as something concrete, immediate, as a condition of life that affects him, threatens him with paralysis of soul. Such being the case, it should be clear as to why Joyce could find no inspiration in a cultural renaissance that found so much of theme and subject in a legendary Irish past. A real Irish presence was far, far too disturbing. Herein is the meaning of a remark Stephen utters in his own defense: "I am not responsible for the past." But, to repeat, he has seen the consequences of that past all about him in the present.

And since this is the case, Joyce is not going to find literary inspiration where the leading literary men of the time found it. He does not have to discover Ireland. He carries too much of it already in his own being.

Moreover, Joyce was born and educated a Catholic. He was trained by Jesuits at the university which Cardinal Newman helped to found. He admired Newman and was influenced by his writings. Behind the lucid prose Joyce saw revealed a man who had arrived at his conviction through spiritual agonies. Stephen is shedding convictions which Newman came to accept, but he, too, is going through spiritual agony in so doing.[3]

From his considerable reading in the literature of the church the boy gained not only a sense of the past but also a sense of an ordered inner world and of a systematized *other* world. Eternity has filled his imagination. Still in his teens, he has been shriveled by fierce fires as he sat in the chapel listening to the Jesuit retreat master describe with rigid logic the physical and spiritual agonies awaiting the damned in hell. (This is one of the most magnificently written passages in all of Joyce's work.) After hearing such sermons Stephen becomes almost physically ill. In fact, this is the period when he suffers most intensely. And his greatest sufferings are not imposed by the Dublin reality which disturbs him so much but by images of an inferno as terrifying as that of Dante. He quivers and cowers

[3] Irony: When the convert, John Henry Newman, later to be cardinal, journeyed to Dublin to deliver his lecture "On the Scope and Nature of a University Education," he could little have dreamed that the most gifted student ever to be graduated from the University he was helping to found would be the author of *Ulysses* and *Finnegan's Wake*.

before the vision of an other world which must make that of the Irish legends seem the most pale of mists. His spiritual struggle is one involving acceptance or rejection of this ordered other world.

He comes to reject it. But his struggle leaves Stephen with a deepened sense of melancholy. He has gained a penetrating sense of the depths of experience. In *Ulysses* Stephen will say that all history is a nightmare. Stephen has known what walking nightmares can be like. He is forging such a temperament that he will never be able to find interest, inspiration, scarcely even curiosity in the ghosts that Yeats sought in castles or in those spirits with whom AE tried to converse. His whole life, his education, his conception of an inner life, all this must lead him to find literary materials different from those that could be shaped by his immediate predecessors. Inasmuch as he is to be a writer, the literary world should presumably be the one aspect of Dublin life where Joyce might find communion of spirit. But this analysis should show how he was gravitating toward a break with this literary world, as with all else in Dublin. The young artist developing before our eyes is one who will be able to feel creatively free only if he directs his eyes toward the future and if he seeks a loveliness not yet born rather than one born centuries ago in Celtic Ireland.

Stephen is the homeless genius. He needs to expand, to feel free. He needs an arena adequate for his talents. He sees no future for himself unless he rebels, rejects. And beyond this Dublin, with its misery, its poverty, its Georgian houses, its sleek patricians, its English rulers, are the cities of the world. Beyond this Ireland, poor and culturally deprived, is the culture of the world. He has felt himself from early boyhood to be different and marked for a special destiny. He cannot and will not participate in politics; he cannot follow the literary men who are making a stir in Dublin. Where can he find a career open for his talents? His feeling of need for expansion and freedom is acute. Are not feelings such as these the kind that were generalized in Ireland's national aspirations? The problems he faces, the needs he feels with the vision of genius—

others have felt, and they have fled. Before him Ireland has had millions of her wild geese sons and daughters. Stephen knows all this. He knows how some have died of starvation; he knows how Tone and Emmet died; and he knows how many have died spiritually.

In terms of all these conditions Stephen's soul is being born. Wherever he turns he sees "nets flung at it to hold it back from flight." But he will be free. The homeless Irishman in Ireland, the homeless genius in the world, he will fly off like Icarus, onward and upward. Proudly rebellious, he has proclaimed: "I will not serve." Instead of the vocation he could not find as a priest, he will find it in service as "a priest of the eternal imagination." Creating without fetters, he will "forge in the smithy of my soul the uncreated conscience of my race." One of Ireland's most brilliant wild geese has found the wings with which he may fly away.

II

In my previous article I discussed James Joyce's *A Portrait of the Artist as a Young Man* in relation to my interpretation of the peculiarities of its Irish setting and historical background. While I consider it important to see the novel placed in this setting, I think it must also be remembered that it belongs not only in modern Irish literature but also in the tradition of the European novel. The *Portrait* presents, in the character of Stephen, an image of the artist. The story depicts how the artist has grown from early childhood to the time in his young manhood when he realizes that his destiny is to be one of dedication to art. In many parts of the narrative the very style in which it is written has direct bearing on the theme. Stephen, feeling so fettered in his native land, sees in art his avenue of escape to freedom.

His conception of art is *fin de siècle*. The influence of Pater on Joyce has often been remarked; Pater's view of esthetics is certainly akin to the attitude toward art which Stephen adopts.

Pater's novel, *Marius the Epicurean*, in fact, seems to be directly related to the *Portrait*. Marius, like Stephen, is being groomed for a life of dedication to an esthetic ideal. Today, when one rereads the *Portrait*, its purple passages seem functional to the content. The prose of *Dubliners*, written before the *Portrait*, is more naturalistic, fresher, simpler; Joyce seems consciously to have adapted his style to his subject matter.

Herbert Gorman in his biography quotes passages of the author's early critical writings. From these, and most especially from his essay on Mangan, it is clear that the young Joyce clothed his ideas on literature in a language strongly resembling that of Pater. He also used many images, concepts, and words that are traditionally considered poetic. When Stephen sees birds in flight, they are described as circling "about a temple of air." When Stephen composes a villanelle, he thinks of the words he has used as "liquid letters of speech. . . ." Poetic words are used consciously and continually. Stephen, as Joyce was always to be, is a word poet, as interested in the sounds of words as in their meaning.

But his language here bespeaks the taste of the time. And it suggests some of Stephen's tastes as much as do any overt remarks concerning literary likes and dislikes. Stephen is something of a dandified esthete of the age. We perceive this even in some of the languorous language that reveals his feelings. But at the same time this languor is altered by his genius, his temperament, his burden of pain, his reactions to the problems he faces. For, although Stephen thinks and feels in this form, he rebels with an anger, a determination, a capacity for resentment that shows him to be a more forceful, a stronger character than, say, Pater's Marius.

Although he is esthetically a rebel, Stephen is strongly respectful of traditions. He does not set out to break with the best traditions of European culture. To the contrary, he seeks to assimilate them, to use them in a way that will aid him in becoming an artist. As I pointed out above, Stephen strongly resents the thinness of Irish culture. He wants a rich culture, a great tradition. When he is set to fly off, he is going to rise not merely from the physical earth of Ireland but also from the cultural earth of western Europe.

His conversations, his reflections indicate that he has already read copiously and that he has learned to assimilate what he has read and to form his own judgments. He forges his own ideas on esthetics, deriving these from the writing of Aristotle and Aquinas. Stephen argues that art effects a purgation in the human consciousness. It cleanses it of all desire, all loathing, all hatreds, all "kinetic" emotions. When one is so cleansed one is elevated and one experiences an "ideal pity and terror," an emotional stasis. The *Portrait* itself is organized on the basis of Stephen's esthetic theory by his successive rejections of a vocation, of family, religion, race, nation. Stephen himself discovers his destiny through a series of spiritual purgations which prepare him to come to art in a spirit of priestly dedication; in fact, he compares the artist to the priest.

Joyce's realism here is a realism of the mind, of the consciousness. Stephen's life is described in a highly concentrated and selective manner, deriving from this point of view. His own mind serves as the frame of reference for the story. Events are revealed to the reader only after they have been assimilated into consciousness and he has stamped his own evaluation upon them. In this way the theme of the novel is developed by a mirroring of successive stages in the change of the hero's consciousness. In addition, not only is a formal theory of esthetics embodied in the narrative but also an act of creation. Stephen shapes his experiences in love into a villanelle, written in the style of Joyce's early poetry. The hero is thus portrayed growing up to become an artist, actively revealing the artistic process by creating a poem, and formally stating his ideas on art. The inner life of the artist is what is significant in his life. Whether or not one may feel that some of the writing is dated, the style, the perspective, the organization of the novel all seem to harmonize beautifully with its content.

The *Portrait* is widely regarded as one of the major modern novels dealing with adolescence and youth. But this view calls for qualifications. Almost from childhood, Stephen is an exceptional character. He is separated from others. He is aloof, lonely, different. His childhood is not a normal one in which he shares the common experiences of give-and-take between boys. He seldom participates in games; he is bookish, introspective. By the time he has become a university student his mind is monkish, cloistered, and he regards it as such. Not only is he superior to his environment, his companions, the members of his own family; he knows he is superior. At the same time he is, until his loss of faith, more tractable than the other boys. His religious faith is deeper than theirs. His pride, his isolation, his difference from others are marked even in his religious emotions. He can perform spiritual exercises, but he cannot really feel a sense of communion with others.

At an opposite pole, he sins alone. He goes to brothels, not in a group but by himself. Instead of discussing his sins with others—something that so many youths do—he embroiders them with languorous and conventionally poetic thoughts. He exists on a higher level of consciousness than others his own age. He does not have real friendships. He carries on one-sided conversations in which, by dominating them, he also reveals himself.

Stephen's temperament is further revealed by the way in which we see him suffer. A great deal of his suffering is described through reflected thoughts and images. His greatest torments come from images, images of the tortures of the damned in hell. When he goes through the pangs of rejected adolescent love, his feelings of shame and humiliation are reproduced, principally, by such a method of reflection. In this respect the *Portrait* is typical of all of Joyce's writing. He rarely describes pain in terms of its immediate impact on characters, and there is little real nervous tension in his world. Usually his characters suffer from the frustration of impulse, loneliness, guilt, shame, the humiliation of pride. When he suffers, Stephen tends to be exceptional as always.

Stephen is not only different from his own peers; he is different from many of the youths of nineteenth-century fiction, for instance, the youths of Tolstoy. No matter how superior a Tolstoy young man may be, he generally goes through the normal experiences of his generation and of his circle. He feels that he belongs in society, and he does what others do, shares experiences and participates in the social life of his class and group. His sensibility may mark him as superior to his comrades, but it does not set him apart from them as Stephen is set apart. But at the same time he is so different. Stephen is a young man who rises out of the tradition of nineteenth-century European literature.

It has often been remarked that in nineteenth-century European fiction the figure of the young man is used to dramatize the problems of the individual set against society and the problems which involve the moral, psychological, and personal consequences of the historic phenomenon known as individualism. Early in the century we see the young man—for instance, Julien Sorel of *The Red and the Black*, or Balzac's Lucien and Rastignac—seek glory and fame. The aim is success, and the plane of action is the objective one of society.

In the Russian novel—Pierre of *War and Peace*, Levin of *Anna Karenina*, Bazarov of *Fathers and Sons*, and Dostoievsky's Raskolnikov and Ivan Karamazov—there is a shift of emphasis. These young men probe for the meaning of life; they seek to harmonize their words and their deeds. And there is still another change of emphasis. We see the young man seeking freedom in the realm of feeling. This is the object of Frederic Moreau in *A Sentimental Education*—and of Des Esseintes (in a purely decadent fashion) in Huysmans' *Against the Grain*. Marius and Stephen are both of this line, and they also seek freedom in the realm of feeling and of culture.

This outline reveals the changing conditions of life in the nineteenth century. The character of public life changes and decreases the opportunities to be free. The idea of culture (as the realm of freedom) begins to grow. Thus, the logic of art for art's sake. The artist, crushed by the weight of contemporary culture, adopts the attitude that art is its own end, becomes the rebel artist. As the rebel, he gives expression to a profound despair that questions the whole moral sensibility of the times.

Such is the despair of a Flaubert, a Rimbaud, a Baudelaire. Stephen is the artist as rebel, questioning the whole moral sensibility of his times. The image of the artist he represents is that of a melancholy but sovereign creator who rises above his times and his own weakness and gazes down with eyes of melancholy at the turgidly flowing river of time, seeking to construct, to mold, to fix in beauty and in sadness that which he sees.

Stephen's ideas of art for art's sake are, further, purposeful ones. In artistic creation he will not only become an unfettered soul. He will also create with a loyalty to a super-personal ideal of the truth. He will try to cast a shadow over the imagination of his race so that he may help them to become more noble. He will strive to forge the conscience of his race, to connect all that produced him with the great streams of European culture. He dedicates himself with pledges of high purpose, and without fears. When he does this, he says: "I do not fear to be alone or spurned for another or to leave whatever I have to leave. And I am not afraid to make a mistake, even a great mistake, a lifelong mistake and perhaps as long as eternity."

It would be pointless to try and discuss the later writing of Joyce in a few final words. *Ulysses* is one of the literary masterpieces of this century, and the impression it has left on world literature promises to be felt for decades to come. Concerning *Finnegan's Wake*, I have made only preliminary efforts to study it, but on the basis of even these attempts, I can say that I strongly disagree with those who attack and denounce it. No writer has ever made such a bold attempt to penetrate the depth and density of man's unconscious mind. Today man on the whole stands in fear of his unconscious mind. But this will not always be so. Man will yet conquer his own unconscious mind as he will society, and when that day comes, all art will be different. I firmly believe that for a new and future art of the fully free man, *Finnegan's Wake* will be considered to have been one of the important books of this age. But it can be said in conclusion that in his later creative life James Joyce kept

Stephen's pledge of dedication. He remains in literature a living inspiration not only because of his great constructive genius, but also because of the living force of his example, his tireless labor, despite his failing eyesight, on major projects, his intensely creative activity, his dignity, his daring, his high artistic courage. Great as is his influence upon the technique of his art, that of his very example is likely to be equally important on writers of the future.

1944

On the Letters of Anton Chekhov

TO EVELYN SHRIFTE

ANTON CHEKHOV[1] was wise in the understanding of the human heart; he was a man of deep humanity. Those who knew him give us much testimony concerning his simplicity of character, his modesty, his gentleness, his kindness, his quiet courage. He was loved by his friends, among whom were Leo Tolstoy and Maxim Gorky. Gorky tells us that once when he and Chekhov were with Tolstoy, the latter sat watching Chekhov, who was walking. Suddenly, Tolstoy turned to Gorky and quietly remarked, "Ah, what a beautiful, magnificent man—modest and quiet as a girl. And he walks like a girl. He's simply wonderful."

But Chekhov's character was not lacking in firmness or in moral strength. A great writer, he had taken the measure of many things in life, and in the face of suffering, he maintained a remarkable poise. For about fifteen years he was a sick man—a dying man. During this time he conducted himself with a dignity that was more than exemplary. He spared his friends the details of his illness, although his ear was open to the troubles of others. A consumptive himself, he was, while at Yalta, continually giving money to fellow sufferers who were poor and he was constantly raising money for them among his friends. Yes, this sick man surveyed his time with sadness, with humanity, with love of his fellow beings. His work is a record of that survey.

[1] In this article, I have quoted from the following books: *Letters of Anton Chekhov to His Family and Friends*, translated by Constance Garnett (New York, 1920); *Reminiscences of Anton Chekhov*, by Maxim Gorky, Alexander Kuprin, and I. A. Bunin, translated by S. S. Koteliansky and Leonard Woolf (New York, 1921); and *Reminiscences of Leo Nikolaevich Tolstoy*, by Maxim Gorky, translated by S. S. Koteliansky and Leonard Woolf (New York, 1920).

I know of no one who has described Chekhov more beautifully than did Gorky: "Banality always found in him a discerning and merciless judge." And he concludes a recollection of Chekhov by describing those characters who populate the Chekhovian world—sad people, gray people, miserable people, men who dream of a noble life three hundred years hence, yet cannot lift a finger to make life more noble and dignified in their own lifetime; women torn and helpless in their love; sisters who see their family go to ruin, yet cannot take one step toward checking the ruin; idle dreamers who live sunk in the commonplace; men and women who cannot react to cruelty, who cannot be free, who cannot lift themselves above the terrible plain of stagnation—people in whom human dignity is dissolving. After describing these characters, Gorky tells us:

"In front of that dreary, gray crowd of helpless people there passed a great, wise, and observant man: he looked at all these dreary inhabitants of his country, and, with a sad smile, with a tone of gentle but deep reproach, with anguish in his face and in his heart, in a beautiful and sincere voice, he said to them: 'You live badly, my friends. It is shameful to live like that.' "

Chekhov raised the portrayal of banality to the level of world literature. He developed the short story as a form of literary art to one of its highest peaks, and the translation of his stories into English has constituted one of the greatest single literary influences at work in the short story of America, England, and Ireland. This influence has been one of the factors encouraging the short-story writers of these nations to revolt against the conventional plot story and to seek in simple and realistic terms to make of the story a form that more seriously reflects life. With the aid of Chekhov's inspiration, some of our own short-story writers have learned to tell us that there is too much dreariness, too much cruelty, too much banality in our own lives. Chekhov has not only influenced the form of the short story, but he has also influenced its content.

Sometimes Chekhov is described as a complete indifferentist. Such an interpretation of him is incorrect. Chekhov was detached, but he was not indifferent. Educated as a doctor, his very training contributed to his detachment. In addition, he was ill—dying—and this protracted illness, which he bore with such fortitude, itself must also have contributed to this detachment. In a letter to a woman, in 1892, a remark of his reveals something of this detachment as it influenced his own writing. He advised her: ". . . when you depict sad or unlucky people, and want to touch the reader's heart, try to be colder—it gives their grief, as it were, a background against which it stands in greater relief." This observation should be treated very seriously by readers, by critics, and by writers. All too frequently the detachment and objectivity of realistic writers is falsely estimated as coldness, even as a lack of humanity. But far from being that, it is often an attitude that enables the writer to save himself from sinking into pits of facile sentimentality.

Chekhov wanted men to be free. In a sense, his stories were a protest that men were not free, because he found them unable to live a more noble and dignified life. In one of his letters he says:

"I should like to be a free artist and nothing more, and I regret that God has not given me the power to be one. I hate lying and violence in all their forms. . . . Pharisaism, stupidity, and despotism reign not in merchants' houses and prisons alone. I see them in science, in literature. . . . My holy of holies is the human body, health, intelligence, talent, inspiration, love, and the most absolute freedom—freedom from violence and lying, whatever forms they may take. This is the program I would follow if I were a great artist."

It is unnecessary to add that Chekhov was a great artist, and that he did follow that program.

Chekhov's comments on literature, in his letters to his friends and his family, help us to understand his work. In some of these letters he has explicitly stated his literary credo. He was a realist. Trained as a doctor, he made no qualitative distinctions between literature and science. To him, both served the same purpose. He conceived the artist and the scientist as specialists, and believed that when each performed his special tasks, he was serving humanity. Underlying these views there was an acceptance of materialism. In a letter to his friend, A. S. Suvorin, written in 1889, Chekhov stated his views on materialism explicitly. Declaring that he cannot understand the reason for crusades against materialism, he says:

"They never lead to anything and only bring needless confusion into people's thoughts. Whom is the crusade against, and what is its object? Where is the enemy and what is there dangerous about him? In the first place, the materialistic movement is not a school or a tendency in the narrow journalistic sense; it is not something passing or accidental; it is necessary, inevitable, and beyond the power of man. All that lives on earth is bound to be materialistic. In animals, in savages, in Moscow merchants, all that is higher and non-animal is conditioned by an unconscious instinct, while all the rest is material, and they, of course, cannot help it. Beings of a higher order, thinking men, are also bound to be materialists. They seek for truth in matter, for there is nowhere else to seek for it, since they see, hear, and sense matter alone. Of necessity they can only seek for truth where their microscopes, lancets, and knives are of use to them. To forbid a man to follow the materialistic line of thought is equivalent to forbidding him to seek truth. Outside matter, there is neither knowledge nor experience, and consequently there is no truth. . . ."[2]

A few days later, he added in another letter:

"Anatomy and belles-lettres are of equally noble descent; they have the same purpose and the same enemy—the devil—and there is absolutely nothing for them to fight about. There is no struggle for existence between them. If a man knows about the circulation of the blood, he is rich; if he also learns the

---

[2] Various realistic and naturalistic writers have differing views on man, nature, and on the social and political problems of their times. But here we can see a suggestion as to what they have in common. They seek to reflect a sense of life, to find the meanings of life in experience itself. However, it does not necessarily follow that they have no values. The task of a critic requires an ability to grasp the values that are often implicit, rather than explicit, in works of literature. Often, however, antinaturalist critics discuss such problems on a literal-minded and purely formal level. It is this literal-mindedness and formality that permit them, from generation to generation, to reiterate the same banalities, the same canards about realists and naturalists.

history of religion and the song "*I Remember a Marvellous Moment,*" he becomes richer, not poorer. . . . It is not branches of knowledge such as poetry and anatomy, but errors—that is to say, men—that fight with one another."

Chekhov's ideal was that of freedom. There is another passage in one of his letters that suggests how he felt realistic literature could greatly assist in the attainment of more freedom:

"Let me remind you that the writers who, we say, are for all time, or are simply good, and who intoxicate us, have one common and very important characteristic. They are going toward something and are summoning you toward it, too, and you feel, not with your mind, but with your whole being, that they have some object. . . . The best of them are realists and paint life as it is, but, through every line's being soaked in the consciousness of an object, you feel, besides life as it is, the life that ought to be, and that captivates you." [3]

In passing, I might add that this passage has on occasion been misused as a justification for attacks on realistic writers by those who possess an antimaterialistic, an antiscientific, bias and see literature as a means of the justification of abstract and generalized moral ideas.[4] Understanding Chekhov's basic ma-

---

[3] "Man will only become better when you make him see what he is like."

[4] Van Wyck Brooks, in *On Contemporary Literature* and *The Opinions of Oliver Allston,* cites this quotation and uses it against the great majority of twentieth-century writers, including some who are not ordinarily described as realists and naturalists. Mr. Brooks makes no effort to explain this quotation in relation to the context of Chekhov's materialism. Besides, he does not analyze this quotation. Chekhov says that writers who are for all time, or are good, are going toward "something." Here "something" is not necessarily that toward which Mr. Brooks is summoning us. Furthermore, the "something" toward which the writers designated are summoning us is not always the same. I think the clearest interpretation of this passage is that great and good writers saturate us with a consciousness of life, and, by achieving this effect, endow us with a sense not only of what life is but also of what it ought to be. This interpretation is one that many realists, past and present, would accept. Mr. J. Donald Adams has also used this quotation from Chekhov for his own purposes, but, like Mr. Brooks, he has not explained it. We see here a clear-cut instance of the intellectual shoddiness of the usual argument for authority. It is rather depressing to realize that many readers and reviewers have not seen through this. Consider this: by saying that writers are summoning us toward "*something,*" you are able to develop an "argument" that dismisses the great majority of important twentieth-century writers of the Western world!

terialism and his advocacy of science, we can see clearly that such a use of this passage is unwarranted.

Chekhov did not take an active part in political life; in fact, his interest in politics was removed, somewhat aloof. He once wrote in a letter: ". . . great writers and artists ought to take part in politics only so far as they have to protect themselves from politics." However, he was far from indifferent to what was happening in Russia. He journeyed across Siberia to study prison conditions in Sakhalin, and wrote of what he saw with the hope of awakening the public conscience in order that penal conditions might be bettered. When an epidemic of cholera threatened to sweep the district in which he lived, he practically abandoned his own work and served without compensation as a zemstvo doctor, traveling about day and night in an effort to check the spread of the plague. When Gorky was not admitted to the Academy, Chekhov resigned from it in protest. He defended the action of Zola in the Dreyfus case; in fact, it was because of this issue that he almost broke off his relations with his friend, the reactionary A. S. Suvorin. Following their correspondence about the case, there was a decided coolness between them. Writing to Suvorin from France, in 1898, he said, ". . . here a new and better Zola has arisen. In his trial he has been cleansed as though in turpentine, from grease-spots, and now shines before the French in his true brilliance. There is a purity and moral elevation that was not suspected in him." In the same letter, he added that Zola would die with a peaceful conscience because of his defense of Dreyfus, and he argued that even were Dreyfus guilty Zola would still have been right, "since it is the duty of writers not to accuse, not to prosecute, but to champion even the guilty once they have been condemned and are enduring punishment." And then he wrote to his brother concerning this disagreement with Suvorin, "I don't want to write and I don't want his letters in which he keeps justifying the tactlessness of his paper by saying he loves the military; I don't want them because I have been thoroughly sick of it all for a long time past . . . to abuse Zola when he is on trial—that is unworthy of literature."

Tolstoy loved Chekhov, and looked upon him as a great artist, as a much finer writer than De Maupassant, whose stories Chekhov himself admired. Chekhov frequently comments on Tolstoy in his letters. In 1900 Tolstoy was severely ill, and it had been expected he might die. Chekhov wrote to M. O. Menshikov:

"His illness frightened me, and kept me on tenterhooks. I am afraid of Tolstoy's death. If he were to die there would be a big empty place in my life. To begin with, because I have never loved any man as much as I have loved him. I am not a believing man, but of all beliefs I consider his the nearest and most akin to me. Secondly, while Tolstoy is in literature it is easy and pleasant to be a literary man; even recognizing that one has done nothing and never will do anything is not so dreadful, since Tolstoy will do enough for all. His work is the justification of the enthusiasms and expectations built upon literature. Thirdly, Tolstoy takes a firm stand, and he has an immense authority, and so long as he is alive, bad tastes in literature, vulgarity of every kind, insolent and lachrymose, all the bristling, exasperated vanities will be in the far background, in the shade. Nothing but his moral authority is capable of maintaining a certain elevation in the moods and tendencies of literature so-called. Without him they would be a flock without a shepherd, or a hotch-potch, in which it would be difficult to discriminate anything."

Gorky felt much the same about Tolstoy, and he wrote, "I am not an orphan on the earth so long as this man lives."

The moral authority of Tolstoy in Chekhov's Russia was immense, and the influence of Tolstoy on all of his contemporaries was incalculable. To Chekhov, Tolstoy's mere physical being was a source of inspiration. But at the same time, Chekhov was critical, even sharply so, of Tolstoy. One of Chekhov's letters contains the following comment on Tolstoy's ideas, which later appeared in *What Is Art?*

"Tolstoy is writing a little book about Art. He came to see me in the clinic, and said that he had flung aside his novel *Resurrection*, as he did not like it, and was writing only about

Art. . . . His idea is not a new one; all intelligent old men in all ages have sung the same tune in different ways. Old men have always been prone to see the end of the world, and have always declared that morality was degenerating to the uttermost point, that Art was growing shallow and wearing thin, that people were growing feebler, and so on, and so on."[5]

And in another letter, he said of these same Tolstoyan ideas: "All that is old. He says about Art that it is decrepit. . . . That's like saying the desire to eat and drink has grown old, has outlived its day, and is not what it ought to be. Of course hunger is an old story; in the desire to eat we have got into a blind alley, but eating is still necessary, and we shall go on eating however the philosophers and irate old men moralize. . . ."

In 1891 he wrote of Tolstoy:

"The devil take the philosophy of the great ones of this world!

[5] *What Is Art?* is an important and frequently misunderstood work. Its basic hypothesis can be retranslated so as to have application today. Briefly, the thesis is that art must be the servant of man rather than man the servant of art. In this book, Tolstoy not only denounced many great works of art in the interest of morality; he denounced the idea of a class art, the exploitation of the masses of the people in the interests and the name of art. Tolstoy was, on more than one occasion, confidently wrong-headed, and there can be no doubt that in this work he pronounced many wrong-headed judgments. At the same time, he is no exception in having done this. Many others in the last years of the nineteenth century and the prewar years of this century also attacked similar tendencies in French literature. Among them was Rosa Luxembourg, who was highly responsive to literature. She attacked the French symbolist movement without really making a full effort to understand its rationale in the given and concrete historic circumstances of its development. Attacks and misunderstandings of this kind suggest that there are definite dangers of mistakes when one deals with literature on the level of personal taste, personal sincerity, personal consciousness of literature, and when one does not, at the same time, see that the problems of literary criticism are also *historical*. In addition to liking and disliking a work, the critic needs to interpret, to recognize, to reveal the *rationale* of literary works and tendencies. To come back to Tolstoy's *What Is Art?*, he revealed in it a serious attentiveness to the cultural needs of the masses. The major mistake he made was that of not clearly seeing that the consciousness of the masses of the people needed to be raised. I hope in the future to discuss Tolstoy's *What Is Art?* in detail. Here I wish to conclude this footnote with the suggestion that a critical reading of *What Is Art?* is something that can well be undertaken at this time, and, if this be done, it should be seen that Tolstoy, unlike some who today caricature this work, did not *solely* attack writers, but what is of more importance, he also denounced the evils of the time, the exploitation of workers and peasants, and the idea of art as being a class prerogative of the educated.

All the great sages are as despotic as generals, and as ignorant and as indelicate as generals, because they feel secure of impunity. . . . Tolstoy abuses doctors as scoundrels, and displays his ignorance in great questions. . . ."

Chekhov was never interested in critics or in formal criticism. He once told Gorky that, after twenty-five years of writing, he had not read one critical piece on his own work that he had found helpful, but that one critic had once predicted that he, Chekhov, would die in a ditch, drunk. However, he usually showed excellent literary taste, and his letters contain many illuminating observations on writers and writing. His advice to young writers was usually generous and helpful, and his letters to the young Gorky are particularly interesting in this respect. There was no snobbery in Chekhov's treatment of young writers; in fact, he often urged others to take a charitable view, arguing that in literature there is room for all honest craftsmen and that those who do even little work—if it be honest—are not to be hounded, attacked, castigated, for, after all, they are not Leo Tolstoy. In his letters, however, I do find but one serious judgment that I think was mistaken, even unfair: his opinion of the great Russian novel *Oblomov* by Gontcharev, of which he said:

"Oblomov himself is exaggerated and is not so striking as to make it worth while to write a whole book about him. A flabby sluggard like so many, a commonplace, petty nature without any complexity in it; to raise this person to the rank of a social type is to make too much of him. I ask myself, what would Oblomov be if he had not been a sluggard? And I answer that he would not have been anything. And if so, let him snore in peace. . . . And the chief trouble is that the whole novel is cold, cold, cold."

These words almost shock one; they read as if they had been written by one of Chekhov's critics instead of by Anton Chekhov. Here Chekhov violates his own doctrine: that it is sufficient for the artist to see life truly, clearly, objectively, and to mirror what he has seen. For *Oblomov* is a profound social study of Czarist Russia in the period before the emancipation of the serfs. Gontcharev, in terms of literature, unmasks the social reasons why sluggards were developed, showing us that Oblomov had to be the son of sluggardly landowners before him, had to have a way of life oozed into his very soul before he could become a classic type and the subject of a great novel. However, a few days after writing this letter, Chekhov wrote of Gontcharev in another: "I am afraid that . . . I resemble Gontcharev, whom I don't like, who is ten heads taller than I am in talent."

I have emphasized the ideas and the comments on literature in Chekhov's letters. But these letters are rich, varied, full of humor, often buoyant in spirit, and they tell us much of his personal life. For many years he was in need of money, and he constantly refers to this need. And his descriptions of what he saw in his travels are tremendously interesting, especially his accounts of his journey across Siberia—the snow-laden steppes, the rivers, the cities, those whom he met. Often, with a simple sentence or two, he reveals a great deal about a place, a city, a person. For instance, he wrote of Paris: "The pavements are filled with little tables, and at the tables sit Frenchmen who feel as though they were at home in the street." Of Monte Carlo, "I love wealth and luxury, but the luxury here, the luxury of the gambling saloon, reminds one of a luxurious water closet."

Of all his letters, those to his wife Olga Knipper,[6] the actress, are the least interesting. He was sick and in his last years when he married her, and they were often separated for long periods of their married life. While he was ill in Yalta, she was often in Moscow, acting with the Moscow Art Theatre. He rarely discussed ideas with her. These letters are filled with details of their constant meetings and separations and with endless references to the weather, to which she, on one occasion, objected. He also wrote of his health, the food he ate, the number of people who came to see him—harassing him, draining him of energy, and thus interfering with his work.

These letters are very matter-of-fact. But they are important

[6] *The Letters of Anton Pavlovitch Chekhov to Olga Leonardovna Knipper*, translated by Constance Garnett (New York, 1924).

if we would understand Chekhov, for they give us a great deal of simple information about the man in his last years. Through them we see not only the great writer, but also the human being so tragically dying. We sense the dreariness of his life on many days when he sat in isolation at Yalta. He wanted to escape from Yalta; he wanted to be in Moscow where there was more life and where the theatre was. He wanted to be where there was more health and vitality. And he was forced to remain in Yalta for long periods. He was wasting away; his energy was running out. He grew more and more detached; at times, his detachment seemed like indifference. It was at this time that he wrote his plays *The Three Sisters* and *The Cherry Orchard*. Just as his letters to his friends chronicle his literary ideas, his tastes, his attitude toward life, so his letters to his wife describe the details of his daily life—when he saw the matron from the girl's school at Yalta, when he visited Tolstoy, when the actor Orlenev came to see him, when the sun was shining, when it was raining, when he received a letter from Stanislavsky, what nights he slept badly, when he had his hair cut and his clothes brushed. Out of these details we build up a picture of the dying author, the great writer grown old too soon because of his illness. We think of him in his chaste room, writing, going into his garden to sit there on sunny days. We note that his poise and his assurance never leave him, and that, as ill as he is, he writes constantly to Olga Knipper and tells her to live well, to work, to be happy. These letters substantiate what Gorky, Kuprin, and Bunin have written about the calm, unruffled, dignified courage with which he faced his illness and met his approaching death. Not even in these last years did he lose his remarkable poise. It was the poise of a man of wit and wisdom, a man who dignified all his human relationships, who gave dignity to all the dreary people about whom he wrote. These letters to Olga Knipper are sad, very sad, not so much because of what they say as because of what they do not say. And yet it was precisely in this period of his decline that Chekhov began to see hope of a new day dawning. He would sometimes tell his friends he was convinced that life in the future would be so much more free, so much more noble than it was in the Russia of the then new century. While he was quietly writing and suffering at Yalta, the mighty forces of the Russian Revolution were gathering, and the winds of this tremendous historic movement blew into the little garden at Yalta and even found themselves reflected in his plays; for instance, in his character Trofimov of *The Cherry Orchard*. And the young Maxim Gorky also brought a breath of these winds with him when he visited Chekhov. Hope grew in the author of alleged hopelessness.

In 1904 Chekhov went to Germany with Olga Knipper. In his last letters to his family we are given no indication of his condition. Less than a month before his death he wrote his sister, "My health has improved. I don't notice now as I go about that I am ill; my asthma is better, nothing is aching. The only trace left of my illness is extreme thinness: my legs are thin as they have never been."

Often life is ironical to the very end. Chekhov died simply, pathetically, troubled by a profound sadness because of the Russo-Japanese war. His body was sent back to Moscow, and, as Gorky and Kuprin have stated, this happened in a truly Chekhovian manner. For, by mistake, it was returned in a car marked "For the Conveyance of Oysters."

Today, the work of Chekhov is part of the great tradition of world literature. It can be said of relatively few men that had they not lived, the world would be spiritually poorer. Anton Chekhov was one such man. And the essential message of his stories and his plays remains the same for us today as it did in his lifetime. What he said then, he now says—with the same pertinency—to many of us, in many countries, and in many languages:

"You live badly, my friends. It is shameful to live like that."

1942

Nonsense and the Short Story

I

IN OUR TIME, perhaps more nonsense has been written about the short story than about any other literary form. Commentators long ago popularized the conceit that the short story is the typical American literary form. There was a time when short stories of a certain plot pattern were in great demand and, for that matter, we are not yet out of that period. The short story has been conceived by persons with "literary" aspirations as a means of making a good living, and it has been used by magazine publishers as bait for procuring advertisements. To use plain language, it has often been employed as a kind of literary pimp. At the present time, scenario writing is viewed as the open sesame for the Get-Rich-Quick-Wallingfords of writing, and the relative commercial rewards of plot short story are less than they used to be.

The short story, then—that so-called typical American literary form—became a business. And just as there are schools to teach accounting, stenography, salesmanship, hotel-keeping, and the like, so there are institutions teaching short-story writing. There are college courses dedicated to this purpose. A whole series of guides to short-story writing—handbooks on the short story, treatises on narrative technique, with special emphasis on the short story, household hints in the production and marketing of the short story, tips, suggestions, charts, outlines, diagrams, maps, and prospectuses—have flooded the market. The libraries are now glutted with such books.

In many instances these books were written in order to keep

flourishing the notion that the art and/or technique of short-story writing could be learned and that, once it was mastered, it could be the means of a profitable and relatively easy livelihood. N. Bryllion Fagin's book, *Short-Story Writing, An Art or a Trade?* (a sincere and clever protest against such tactics), points out clearly that the ease of mastering the short-story technique (so-called) was stressed because of such reasons. By doing this, the teachers were helping to give their own business the status of a going concern. Mr. Fagin quotes one of the instructors of this business as follows: "Given a reasonable intelligence and a sufficient patience, any man with the smallest gifts may learn to write at least marketable stuff, and may earn an honest livelihood, if he studies the taste of the least exacting portion of the public, and accommodates himself to the whim of the time." The late Blanche Colton Williams, former head of the Department of English at Hunter College, City of New York, was one of the practitioners of this form of literary advice-mongering. In the preface of her book, *A Handbook on Story Writing,* she writes: "The story is so much a matter of form, it can be learned. Conceivably it can be learned by persons who are endowed with no supreme literary gift." Nor has this business and its practices been confined to this country alone. Thus, an Englishman, Cecil Hunt, tells us in *Short Stories, How to Write Them* that "Short-story writing is not easy money; it is not a fool's game; but, given the . . . qualities" of a desire to write, average capacity, enthusiasm, etc., "it can be learned as easily as most other occupations. It gives a higher return in money and in pleasure than many. What is more, it can be a delightful and remunerative hobby."

Upon examination, most of the short-story handbooks are to be seen largely as expansions and extensions of what the late Brander Matthews wrote some years ago in his *The Philosophy of the Short-story.* And it must be added that he wrote next to nothing of real literary worth, insight, or suggestiveness. He placed his emphasis on form, and thus he said: "The Short-story is nothing if there is no story to tell." And again: "A Short-story in which nothing happens at all is an absolute impossibility."

He distinguished between the short story and the sketch, stating that "while a Sketch may be an outline of character, or even a picture of a mood of mind, but in a Short-story there must be something done, there must be action." When he branched off to speak of content, he was downright silly. For instance, take this priceless observation: "While the Novel cannot get on easily without love, the Short-story can."

To repeat, most of the latter-day books on short-story writing are largely derivative from Matthews. They follow his definitions and demarcations of the story in terms of form. But that is only a prelude, a breaking of ground for the real stuff— the charts, the formulas, the outlines, the plot diagrams, the analyses of methods of obtaining effects, the breaking up of narrative techniques into its assumedly component parts, the presentation of an entire cabalistic ritual of writing. For example, there is one Stewart Beach, former Lecturer on Short-story Writing at New York University. In his book, *Short-story Technique,* he outlines a method that is particularly important for the neophyte. This is his "X-ray method," which, he says, "demands unity of focus" and "is an ingeniously simple scheme which depends for its success upon the author's borrowing one leaf from the book of the theater and another from the clinical notes of the doctor. Instead of *telling* [italics in original] a story about a group of characters or about something which happened to some one, the author places one character under the X-ray and allows his readers to see his thoughts as well as his actions." He talks about "snares" to catch the reader's interest; tells us that the short story has a beginning, a body, and an ending; asks and learnedly discusses such questions as: "How is the author to know the actual point at which the beginning ends and the action shifts over into the body of the story?" He comments on the "piecemeal method of introducing exposition" and informs us that there are four essentials in plot building: "chief actor"; "basic characteristic" of the chief actor; "original situation"; "problem." He discusses the "mechanics of suspense" and points out that suspense grows from two roots: conflict and contrast. He lists the simple types of conflict under five headings: man with himself; man with his background; man with his situation; man with man; man with fate. Blanche Colton Williams goes him one better and catalogues six types of struggle (or conflict) : beast with beast; man with beast; man with natural forces; man with man [under which heading there are subcategories from a to g]; man with fate; man with supernatural forces. Beach's remarks in this connection are sufficiently momentous to warrant quotation: "Contrast is the stuff of conflict, but conflict is the stuff of *suspense*." (Italics in original.)

Then there is Professor E. A. Cross, whose *A Book of The Short Story* is full of a cabalistic lore all its own. Professor Cross goes to the heart of the matter by asking the question: what kinds of people should the short-story writer use? He answers, "In the first place, the characters must be real people." And he states that there are two methods of delineating character: "direct" and "indirect." His most notable contribution to this esoteric science, however, is to be found in his diagrams of plots. He is the man who has demonstrated the plot diagrams of stories. Thus, *The Piece of String* has a "stair-step" plot, and many of O. Henry's plots, when diagrammed, are of the "rocket" design.

It is to be noticed in all these views that something called *form* is stressed. In other words, it can be said that the positive value here is that of *structure*. The philosophy of the short story, as outlined, is one in which structure is given positive value. Upon examination we discover here the weakness in all approaches to literature that are purely formal. This kind of form becomes a philosophy, a value. In the traditional American short story, this is precisely what has happened. A writer whose sole gift is technical facility will rise to the top, be greatly overrated, and his work will be cited as an inspiration for beginners. Thus the reputation of a writer such as Wilbur Daniel Steele is explained. His sole capacity is that of technical facility; for the rest, he is sterile. In my opinion he is the example par excellence of the writer whose only positive value is form, structure. When form and structure in this way become predominant values in literature, the material from life, on which literature draws, is falsified. Inevitably there is a loss of concern with content. Content is altered—but not to gain that more concentrated effect and meaning which literature strives to achieve. It is changed, pieced together, in order to make it fit into an arbitrary structure. Life is falsified. A literature of hollow and straw men is produced.

It was Edward James O'Brien, I believe, who suggested there was a peculiar faith in predestination to be found in the conventional and traditional conceptions of the American short story. He analyzed this phenomenon, however, as a product of the machine age and of the standardization that develops in such an epoch. Here he tended to focus the questions within the confines of an arbitrary perspective. We find semblances of such an attitude in his books, *The Advance of the American Short Story* and *The Dance of the Machines* (which discusses the short story at some length). He polarizes man and the machine. According to his view, the standardization of the machine age has produced the standardized machine story. He neglected to realize that in previous epochs—before there was what properly can be called a machine age—writing was often equally as conventionalized as it has been in the representative American plot short story. Before the romantic movement in English letters, there was standardization—the result, largely, of neo-classicism. In French painting there was a similar type of conventionalization. It was broken by Delacroix and other predecessors of the Impressionists, and then, more decisively, by the Impressionists themselves.

So the analogy with the machine is an unsatisfactory explanation of this phenomenon. The growth of science, on which the machine is based, has done more to liberate than it has to mechanize literature.[1] However, Mr. O'Brien's suggestion that the traditional American short story exemplifies an inclination toward a faith in predestination is, to repeat, suggestive. To

[1] Obviously the real problem is that of who owns the machine, and for what purpose the machine is put to use. Mr. O'Brien, like so many others who have written on this subject, has posed questions which conceal the real issue involved.

cite the best example that comes to mind, I shall have to go outside of the technical limits of the short story and examine a novelette, *The Go-Getter*, by Peter B. Kyne. Herein we find a typical illustration of the American faith in go-getting as it is incorporated into a story pattern. The outlook implicitly inculcated into the very pattern and movement of the story is that go-getting is automatically bound to bring success. Success is conceived in financial terms. The story contains a definite moral, or theme. If you try, if you won't allow yourself to be licked, if you bend every effort toward doing your job in business—you will rise. You will be a financial success. You will move up the ladder. Also, of course, there is the additional suggestion that with this kind of effort and with the success that results from it, you will also obtain a wife. Professor Beach states that the "necessity of a definite conclusion" in the short story "naturally presupposes a story for which such a conclusion is possible." The conventional short story has been reduced largely to a proposition in a priori problem-solving. In this sense it affirms an essentially Calvinistic faith in predestination.

Calvinism furnished the rising capitalism of another century with a religious justification. It served to bring the form of religion, a modification of, a mutation upon, medieval Christianity, into harmony with a rising capitalism. The ideological background of the conventional American short story has one of its main sources here. This form has now reached the stage of development where its positive affirmation, its implied view, is merely that of structure. This structure delimits the literary form and demands that certain things be done with characters and events that are utilized in this form. The content poured into this structure has been mainly of a kind that implicitly or explicitly affirms and enforces an acceptance of the aims and ideals that are part of the ideological structure of capitalism. One of the products of the rise of capitalism and the ascension to power of the bourgeoisie as a class has been the development of a sense of the self and of the individual that is totally different from the view of the individual that prevailed in earlier epochs, such as those of the medieval and classic civilizations. With the Renaissance, the rise of the middle class, and the development of modern science, a new view of the self came into the consciousness of men on a wholesale scale. Self-consciousness, as we know it today, developed. Man began to trust more and more to his own nature, his own impulses, his own resources and knowledge. Man began to view himself as self-dependent. Freedom of action in various fields of endeavor flows from this view of the self, and a constituent of that freedom of action is freedom to buy and to sell.

Individualism in this more limited sense is the individualism that very often has been inculcated into the traditional American short story. The content of many such stories is formed from a simplified view of individualism. The individual is conceived as the best judge of his own wants. He must rely on himself. His future depends on what he does. If he is a go-getter, if he adheres to the prevailing views of life and seeks the "worthy" goods of life, if he plays the game of capitalistic struggle, he will advance. He will be a success. Success will bring happiness.

Such is the typical content of many traditional American short stories. In others, there is a treatment of a related nature. Or there is a local-color content that tends to patronize those who are of a lower economic origin or of a "socially inferior" race. One may cite as stories of the latter type the Octavius Roy Cohen series featuring Florian Slappey. Added to this simple type of individualism there is a hygienic and largely hypocritical morality and a carry-over of the virgin complex that traces back to the medieval cult of the virgin. The ideal of life is success, and the fruits of success are marriage to an American virgin, a home in the suburbs that contains all the advantages, conveniences, gadgets, automobiles, radios, etc., that are to be found advertised in the magazines that have long specialized in printing precisely this type of story.

And while the plot short story has been driven backward into a succession of retreats, not all the effects of its earlier acceptance have been dissipated. For instance, the view of structure that enshrines it as a positive value persists in the drama today. Play structure in some instances is elevated almost into a philosophy forming the basis for interpreting characters and events. Similar influences are being brought back into the stream of American literature through the medium of Hollywood. The same influences are still at play in the minds of masses of Americans. As a result, the appreciation not only of the short story, but also of all forms of literature, is deadened. The view of the short story in formal terms is still retained in whole or in part by many who consider themselves sophisticated book reviewers, critics, editors. One way this is done is by dodging the task of appreciating and interpreting short stories by posing irrelevant questions. Is this specific work a short story? Are these particular pieces of fiction short stories, or are they not? Such a question is easily asked. It is an excellent question for the critic or reviewer who seeks to pad his review, to avoid appreciating a work, judging it, evaluating it. Several paragraphs, or even pages, can be spun around it, and then the critic can remark that the particular work or works are, or are not, short stories. Thanks largely to the popularity of writers such as Joyce and Proust, it is difficult for critics to employ the same subterfuge in discussing a novel. Consequently, there is a greater tendency to measure the short story in a formal manner than there is to measure the novel in this way. This tendency, of course, is largely a hangover from the days when the plot short story was leading the field.

II

We come now to the question: "What is a short story?" There are definitions piled on top of other definitions, and I shall cite some. Professor Beach, the apostle of "the X-ray method" of writing short stories, has this definition: "The short story, in so far as its scope is concerned, is the simplest form of fiction. Unlike the novel, it lacks space to unfold a complex situation." John T. Frederick, editor of the defunct *Midland*, has written one of the more intelligent books in this field, *A Handbook of Short Story Writing*, although he, too, gives some of the usual synthetic advice on narrative technique and the like. He says: "The aim of short story writing must be no longer defined in terms of approximation of artificial canons of form and method, but primarily in terms of the sincerity of the writer and the significance of his material." Professor Cross, he who seems to have invented the "stair-step" and the "rocket" plot diagrams, says: "Like the novel, the short story is a piece of fiction producing a unified effect. Unlike the novel, the single effect is usually an *impression* [italics in original] instead of a deliberate marshaling together of a large number of diverse elements into a unity. . . . The short story is a cross section of life . . . but of a single life or at most of the thread of life where it crosses and becomes entangled with one or two other subordinated threads—a section through the knot." Professor Cross also quotes Clayton Hamilton, another adept at this recondite wisdom, who says, in his *A Manual of the Art of Fiction: "The aim of a short-story* [italics in original] *is to produce a single narrative effect with the greatest economy of means that is consistent with the utmost emphasis."* Edith Mirrielees, who is the author of *Significant Contemporary Stories*, and is quoted by Blanche Colton Williams, states: "In the first fraction of the twentieth century, a short story is a fiction in prose of a somewhat limited magnitude—that and no more." In her book, *Writing the Short Story*, Miss Mirrielees gives this definition: "*A short story is a brief prose narrative, primarily imaginative, which, by means of the adhesion of every part to one central purpose, renders a coherent and interpretative account of some phase of action, character, or mood."* [Italics in original.] Blanche Colton Williams (whose own book bears out the ironical remark of Edward James O'Brien: that most of the handbooks are like treatises on bridge building because of their charts and diagrams) of course has her definition: "The short story is a prose narrative artistically presenting character in a struggle or complication which has a definite outcome. If the action occurs in a brief time and a closely circumscribed space, the story approaches the extreme or ultimate form." Which of these definitions is best suited to the stories of Chekhov—in my opinion the greatest short-story writer who ever lived? Or which one is most applicable to the stories in Joyce's *Dubliners*? To *Winesburg, Ohio*? Amen. and again— amen!

To anyone concerned with the evaluation and appreciation of literature, it is not crucial whether a particular work be a novel, a condensed novel, a novelette, a story, a tale, a sketch, an anecdote, an incident, a dramatic dialogue, or whatever other term be applied. What does matter is whether a specific piece of writing provides the reader with an *experience*, whether it increases his or her understanding, intensifies his or her consciousness, provides the reader with pleasure and refreshment. All the definitions with which I am familiar are arbitrary. And when we refer them to our actual experience in reading, we readily perceive how arbitrary they are. For instance, some of the experts tell us that the short story creates a *single* or a *unified* impression. What is the meaning here of "single"? Of "unified"? When we look at a work of art, we learn that there are not just *single* impressions to be gathered from it. If we take a story such as Chekhov's "A Woman's Kingdom," what is the single and unified impression we gain from reading it? This is a story of class relationships in Czarist Russia and it is, literally, a cross section of many phases of the life of that place and period. One gets from it impressions of class relationships, of characters, of moods. What, then, of the singleness of impression? In fact, Chekhov's stories are an excellent refutation of all these definitions. His stories are, in my opinion, like doors of understanding and awareness opening outward into an entire world. How, then, can we speak of the *single* impression they create? Perhaps this will explain why a pundit once boasted that Chekhov wrote sketches, but that we, Americans, write short stories. What we can see here is really the nonsense of the short-story pundits. However, it is needless to stress that it has been a very profitable nonsense.

1937

How Studs Lonigan *Was Written*

I

I BEGAN WRITING what has developed into this trilogy in June, 1929. *Judgment Day* was finally completed at the end of January, 1935. In June, 1929, I was a young man who had burned other bridges behind him with the determination to write, whether my efforts brought me success or failure. I was then finishing what happened to be my last quarter as a student at the University of Chicago. Three times before I had dropped out of classes because I was restless and dissatisfied, resolved to devote my time to writing and to educating myself in my own haphazard manner. For a fourth and last time I had matriculated and I managed to finish the quarter. Although I read continuously and rather broadly, after my sophomore year I could not maintain a steady interest in any of my courses except in composition, where I could write as much as I pleased. I would cut other classes, day after day, finally dropping out, heedless of the loss of credit and the waste of money I had spent for tuition.

My mood and state of mind in those days were, I believe, of the kind which most young writers will recognize. To be a young man with literary aspirations is not to be particularly happy. At first, the desire to write is more strong than is a clear perception of what one wants to write and how one will write it. There are surprising oscillations of mood. One moment the young writer is energetic and hopeful. The next he is catapulted into a fit of despair, his faith in himself infirm, his self-

it becomes a nostalgic image turned toward the past. Does this not happen in greater or lesser degree to all of us?

Shortly after I began working on *Studs Lonigan,* I happened to be reading John Dewey's *Human Nature and Conduct,* and I came upon the following sentence which I used as a quotation in *Young Lonigan:* "The poignancy of situations which evoke reflection lies in the fact that we do not know the meaning of the tendencies that are pressing for action." This observation crystallized for me what I was seeking to do. This work grew out of a situation which evoked reflection. The situation revealed to me the final meaning of tendencies which had been pressing for action. And that final situation became death, turning poignancy into tragedy. *Studs Lonigan* was conceived as the story of an American destiny in our time. It deals with the making and the education of an ordinary American boy. My attitude toward it and toward my character here is essentially a simple one. "There but for the grace of God go I." . . . There but for the grace of God go—many others.

1938

Literature and Ideology

WHAT IS THE RELATIONSHIP between literature and politics? What should that relationship be? Such questions have produced major literary controversies in this country for more than a decade. About ten years ago these questions were central in the discussion of so-called proletarian literature. Today, these same issues are being discussed in connection with literature and democracy and literature and the war. In current discussions the language is different from what it was ten years ago, but both those who were the apostles of proletarian literature and those who today demand that literature be politicalized in the name of democracy have something in common: in both instances the aim is to compel the writer to abort his work in the name of *formal* political ends and to impose critical and political legislation on him.

The advocates of proletarian literature, who wrote principally in *The New Masses*, used to argue that literature is a weapon in the class struggle. If the writer is not on one side, he is either an open defender of the enemy or else he is giving aid and comfort to that enemy. At times it was even claimed that literature itself was on the barricades. These views were advocated in a formal and sectarian spirit, and behind them was the *real aim* of bureaucratizing literature so that it would become merely the docile handmaiden of politics, of ideology, even of a specific party line.[1] The writer who accepted this conception

[1] I have discussed in detail my own views on some of these questions in *A Note on Literary Criticism*. Views directly counter to my own are to be

90

and attempted to make it operative in the actual construction of novels would have to see politics first and then life, and he would have to deduce life from political programs. To the theoreticians of proletarian literature the theme of a book was considered its most important, its most essential, element: the total

---

found in *The Great Tradition,* by Granville Hicks. There are a number of books which relate to this question and in various ways. I cite a few of them: *Literature and Revolution,* by Leon Trotsky; *Voices of October,* Joseph Freeman, Joshua Kunitz, and Louis Lozowick, editors; *American Writers' Congress,* Henry Hart, editor; *The Destructive Element,* by Stephen Spender; *The Triple Thinkers,* by Edmund Wilson; *Problems of Soviet Literature,* by A. Zhdanov, Maxim Gorky, N. Bukharin, K. Radek, and A. Stetsky; *The Liberation of American Literature,* by V. F. Calverton; *Illusion and Reality,* by Christopher Caudwell; *Artists in Uniform* and *Art and the Life of Action,* by Max Eastman; *Forces in American Criticism,* by Bernard Smith, *La Littérature et l'Art, choisis, traduits et présentés par* Karl Marx *et* F. Engels; *Art and Society,* by George V. Plekhanov (introduction by Granville Hicks). In Ireland, during the period of national revolutionary ferment, prior to the Easter Rebellion of 1916, the same question was discussed in literary controverises, but there it was an issue concerning literature and the aspirations of the nationalist movement. One who defended the writer against the criticisms of the nationalists —those who demanded that Anglo-Irish literature serve as a direct political instrument of the national movement—was the Lord Mayor of Cork, the late Terence MacSwiney (cf. *Principles of Freedom*). MacSwiney stated: "It is because we need the truth that we object to the propagandist playwright." It is important to stress that these bureaucratically politicalized views on literature were presented in a formal and abstract manner, with utter heedlessness of conditions, of class relationships, of states of consciousness in America during the 1930's, when these opinions were more strongly and widely presented. It was generally impossible for a writer to make the bridge between these formal claims for literature and the character and quality of his own experience. By and large, life in America did not seem at all like the insistences as to what life should be like according to these formally asserted views on proletarian literature, and the claims that literature itself was on the barricades. The tactics (it was tactics, not strategy) of politics were applied to the practices of literature, which deals with the consciousness of men. This can be seen clearly if we consider that frequently—and especially in poetry and verse during the early thirties—slogans were used in poetry. One of these slogans was that which Lenin used in the period between the February and October Revolutions in Russia: "All Power to the Soviets." This slogan did not at all correspond to the general state of consciousness of the American workers during the early 1930's, and that, in addition, if at that time this slogan had been made a central slogan politically, it would have led to disastrous adventurism, to *putschism,* to the most terrible defeat of the American working class. This slogan, politically untimed, was bad when used in many poems and verses. At that time scarcely one per cent of the entire population of America understood, even in the most elementary sense, what the Soviets really were, theoreti-

pattern of a novel, its unfoldment of characters and events, its insights, which help to clarify for us the mysteries of man and his world, and its very style—these were all relegated to a secondary place. A true re-creation of social relationships and of human beings was considered to be less important than the

cally or practically. Many critics of Marxism have never taken the trouble to study the problems involved in the study of literature in its relationships with politics, and in terms of its functions in society. Hence they cite the efforts of the Marxist and of the so-called Marxist critics of the early 1930's as proof that Marxism is harmful to literature. They accept formal, abstract, even utterly lifeless, expositions, and even caricatures of Marxian thought, as fair statements; and they then refute, or try to refute, these formal statements. If one writes to emphasize the veritable truism that you cannot seriously judge literature if you make it the simple handmaiden of ideology, of political tactics, of economics formally and abstractly considered, such critics often assume that you are thereby abandoning Marxism. The grievous mistakes of critics who call themselves Marxists do not excuse the ignorance of their adversaries. The errors of the former do not establish the validity of the arguments of the latter. In general, in the early 1930's, the proponents of proletarian literature wrote with almost total irrelevance to the real situation in America, to the real states of consciousness of writers, and their readers, and to the types of characters depicted in the novels and stories then written. Mistaken, bureaucratically imposed, politically motivated applications of hypotheses do not furnish a necessary and sufficient refutation of these hypotheses. Finally, when critics and others demand that literature—art—be politicalized, there is a reason, a motive for this. Such demands imply or even explicitly reveal political aims and intentions, and the successful implementation of such demands produce consequences. In discussing such demands one needs to remember these truisms, and to consider them most carefully. In the case of the demand for proletarian literature, it should be remembered that most of those who made such demands were incapable of practicing what they preached, either critically or creatively, and, furthermore, that the political achievements claimed as possible on the basis of the political strategy and tactics that motivated this literary approach were never realized. Before one can, with real grounds, refute Marxism in general on the basis of the claims of the so-called Marxist critics of the early thirties, one must consider and evaluate both the political and the literary "lines" then in vogue. This is not usually done by critics. The real consequence of this line was that it prepared the road for a later politicalization or attempted politicalization of art, that which is in vogue today. The tendencies revealed in the recent writings of Van Wyck Brooks, Archibald MacLeish and others have a political character, and can, if successful, only end in an official art. And these tendencies are intimately related to the present war; in fact, they are involved as part of a general metaphysics of the war. A primary basis for a metaphysics of the war is the creation of what amounts to a metaphysics of the cause of the war. The present efforts to politicalize literature, to officialize it, are part of this effort: this is their *real politics*.

merely formal ideology that was implanted into a novel and openly affirmed in the last chapter. The ending was stressed as against the entire story and its legitimate meanings and implications. Most of the great writers of the present and of the past were attacked, often severely, as bourgeois defeatists; and in their place novelists such as Jack Conroy, Arnold Armstrong, William Rollins, and others were hailed as the inheritors not only of the literary traditions of America but also of those of the whole world.

In this article it is not necessary for me to go into historical detail or to discuss this point of view at length. Those who sponsored it have themselves abandoned all their claims. They have themselves forgotten most of the authors they lauded as proletarian writers, and they now praise the writers whom they then attacked—for instance, Thomas Mann. And most of the young writers who adopted this view of literature have themselves stopped writing. If a conception of literature produces no books, then it is obvious that that conception is defective. It remains sterile and formal. If the most rigid supporters of a conception abandon it, regardless of the reason, it is not necessary for me to refute here what they themselves have already refuted in the most positive manner.

It is ironical to observe that some of the writers who defended the complete freedom of the writer from politics in the early 1930's are now included in the vanguard of the newest group of politico-critical legislators; they now demand that the creative artist adopt the same type of approach that they themselves once attacked, even heatedly. The popular writers whose work appears in the slick magazines and who receive large sums from Hollywood are also included in this vanguard.[2]

2 *Pitfalls for Readers of Fiction,* by Hazel Sample, a pamphlet published by the National Council of Teachers of English, contains an able analysis of certain types of popular fiction and of the assumptions on which these are based. The most vulgar of those who would force literature to become official have even gone to the extent of hailing motion pictures—similar in content, basic assumptions, and in emphasis on escape values, to the novels studied by Miss Sample—as greater contributions to American culture and the fight for a free world than serious works of American realism that try to describe conditions and characters truly. For instance, Mr. Strunsky, who writes the "Topics of the Times"

POSITIONS OF MACLEISH AND BROOKS

A leading exponent of this tendency is Archibald MacLeish. (*Cf.* Archibald MacLeish, *The Irresponsibles.*) During the height of the bitter polemical controversy concerning prole-tarian literature, Mr. MacLeish was moved to write in defense of complete freedom of the poet. In those days he believed the poet should merely sing. And some of *The New Masses* critics did not stop at describing Mr. MacLeish as irresponsible—they called him a fascist. Today Mr. MacLeish has reversed himself, and he sharply criticizes almost all modern writers as irresponsibles. His major charge is that, during a period of growing danger to the entire human race, they merely tried to see life truly and to create honest pictures of life. They did not defend ways of thinking, ideas and beliefs that should have been defended. They did not use the word as a weapon with which to storm the barricades of belief; and consequently, they contributed to the demoralization of democratic forces, with the result that this demoralization left democracy in a weakened state at a time when it must defend itself against a sinister enemy. It is inter-esting to note in passing that the one writer whom MacLeish excepts from his blanket condemnation is Thomas Mann—and it is on record that many of the writers implicitly or openly attacked by MacLeish took a stand on the question of fascism before Thomas Mann would openly condemn the Hitler regime. Further, there is a stream of pessimism in the books of Thomas Mann that makes the assertions of MacLeish appear somewhat ridiculous.

Another person who has now adopted a position analogous to that of MacLeish is the critic Van Wyck Brooks. (*Cf.* Van Wyck Brooks, *On Contemporary Literature* and *The Opinions of Oliver Allston.*) Mr. Brooks believes that modern

---

column for the *New York Times,* has declared that serious American realists give us nothing to fight for, but that the escape movies of Hollywood do give us something we can fight and die for. In other words, the simple, tragic, spiritually impoverished people described in American realistic novels are not worth fighting for; but it is proper to die for Tyrone Power and his world.

writers are cynics and that they write out of hatred and a drive-toward-death. They have, he asserts, lost the idea of greatness, and inasmuch as they themselves are not great men, they cannot write great books. Excepted from this charge are Robert Frost, Lewis Mumford, Waldo Frank, Archibald Mac-Leish, and Thomas Mann. Modern writers—and Mr. Brooks makes no distinctions between various modern literary tendencies, including that of realism and that of radical experimentalism stemming from the French symbolists—have lost their connection with the soil. They have no roots in the region, in the country, or in its soil. In passing, it may be observed that this conception is, in essence, Spenglerian. Consequently, it is startling to see that Mr. Brooks, in his little book, *On Contemporary Literature,* charges that modern writers have been influenced by Spengler, including those—such as the author of this article—who have for years been anti-Spenglerian. Furthermore, one of the European novelists of the soil, with roots in the soil, is Knut Hamsun, who was one of the first world-famous literary figures to become a fascist.

Mr. Brooks claims that modern writers write demoralizing books because they have no attachment to the family and because they do not take an interest in public life. On both of these points he is unspecific. He does not demonstrate in a concrete manner precisely how a writer will become a better artist by transplanting himself to the country and living close to the soil, by declaring an attachment to the family (most writers are attached to their families, love them, and try to support them), and by taking an open interest in public life. In addition, he is not specific concerning the manner in which a writer should become interested in and attached to public life. Should he take a political stand on issues? Should he run for an elective office? Should he abandon literature and dedicate himself to political theory or to political polemics? Should he ghost-write speeches for political leaders? And, incidentally, some of the writers whom Brooks accuses of lacking an interest in public life have been far more politically active on many issues than he has. In essence, Brooks is adopting the same general attitude toward

literature as did his recent forebears, the apostles of proletarian
literature, even though he clothes his views in a concealing dress
of moralism. Like them, he and Archibald MacLeish and others
are seeking to legislate for writing, to tell the writer what to
do, what to write, what ideology to inculcate through his works,
what conclusions to come to in a novel, and what to think.

ITS RELATION TO POLITICS

Those who adopt such an approach toward literature do not
clearly focus the problems of literature, the nature of writing,
the functions and purposes that literature can perform. When
Karl Marx was a young man, editing a democratic newspaper
in the Rhineland and working toward the point of view which
he finally adopted and developed, he wrote a letter to a friend
which contains some remarks that are today a pertinent and
decisive answer to the claims of those who would *sneak* politics
and ideology into literature. At that time Marx had not yet
been converted to socialism. He resisted the pressure of philosophical and literary friends who took a frivolous attitude
toward serious questions, and he explained why he rejected the
articles of these people. He wrote:

"I demanded less vague arguments, fewer fine-sounding
phrases, less self-adulation and rather more concreteness, a more
detailed treatment of actual conditions and a display of greater
practical knowledge of the subjects dealt with. I told them that
in my opinion it was not right, that it was even immoral, to
smuggle communist and socialist dogmas, that is, an entirely
new way of looking at the world, into a casual dramatic criticism, etc., and that if communism were to be discussed at
all then it must be done in quite a different fashion and
thoroughly."

Today, as then, literary men are trying to smuggle ideology
into literature. "Smuggle" is an excellent word here. They
seek to consider, to discuss, and to educate people in an indirect,
oblique, yes, even casual, manner concerning the most serious

problems confronting the human race. Instead of discussing questions such as socialism and communism, democracy and fascism, in terms of the relevant problems raised by those issues, they want to smuggle a discussion of such issues into novels, poetry, dramatic criticisms, book reviews, motion picture scenarios, cheap swing songs, soap operas, banquet speeches, and books labeled as literary criticism. I do not hesitate to characterize such conduct as frivolous; often it is positively immoral. Politics is serious. It is the arena in which the fundamental bread-and-butter struggles of men, of groups, of nations, of social classes are conducted. He who is frivolous about politics is guilty of a grave disservice to his fellow men, especially in times of deep social crisis. The problems of politics are basically concerned with action and with power. Literary men have the habit of rushing into the periphery of politics and they contribute to political struggles—not knowledge, not practical experience, not theoretical analyses, but rhetoric. Rhetoric is the one commodity in politics of which there has never been a scarcity.

My subject, however, is not the political conduct of literary men in politics. I do not criticize this *per se*. I merely suggest that the requisites of all responsible action are that one be serious and that one accept the obligations and duties which that endeavor imposes on one. My concern here is with the efforts to politicalize literature. The final result of the politicalization of literature can only be an official, or state, literature. The extreme example of a state, or official, literature in our times is that of the totalitarian countries. It need not be commented upon in this article. We know what it is and what it leads to and how it destroys genuine literature in the most brutal and ruthless fashion. It is possible to silence writers by force; a state power can put writers into jail and treat them as common criminals; it can prevent publication of their books; it can execute them. However, it cannot, either by open force or by offering prizes, praise, awards, or academic and institutional honors, make them write good books. Modern authoritarian rulers are not the first ones who have been taught this elementary lesson. But literary men often fail to learn it. During the period of the Second Empire, even the great critic Sainte-Beuve was ready to play along with the idea of an official literature. The attempt to create an official literature in that period failed. Two of the greatest French writers of the times, Flaubert and Baudelaire (both friends of Sainte-Beuve), were haled to court on censorship charges.[3] The poetry of Baudelaire was suppressed. Today we read Flaubert and Baudelaire but not the official writers of Louis Bonaparte.

Napoleon Bonaparte still remains the greatest of modern dictators. Himself a gifted writer and a man who developed literary taste through the course of his lifetime, he tried to impose an official art and literature on France when he was its ruler. In the year 1805 he wrote to Fouché, who was then Minister of Police:

"I read in a paper that a tragedy on Henry IV is to be played. The epoch is recent enough to excite political passions. The theater must dip more into antiquity. Why not commission Raynouard to write a tragedy on the transition from primitive to less primitive man? A tyrant would be followed by the savior of his country. The oratorio *Saul* is on precisely that text—a great man succeeding a degenerate king."

In the same year he wrote: "My intention is to turn Art specially in the direction of subjects that would tend to perpetuate the memory of the events of the last fifteen years." He justified expenditures for opera on the ground that it flattered the national vanity. A year later he confessed that his official opera had only degraded literature and the arts, and he demanded that something be done to halt the degradation caused by his own official policies and his control of the opera. Then he declared: "Literature needs encouragement." Something had to be proposed to "shake up the various branches of literature that have so long distinguished our country." But literature did not distinguish France during the period of *la gloire*. The writer was told to behave—and generally he obeyed orders. The chief of

---

[3] The history of literature for decades now teaches us that it is not unlikely for serious writers to win the merit of having gained the solicitude of the police power.

police and the ministers of the cabinet gave him instructions as to what to write, and they honored him for obeying instructions. But Napoleon himself was forced—after all, he was a man of some taste—to show contempt for his own official litterateurs. In exile at Saint Helena, he did not read them. He did not speak of them. He remembered Racine, and he remembered Homer, but he remembered no literature that could distinguish his own period of rule. And neither do we today remember any of it. Is more eloquent demonstration of the failure of this attitude toward literature needed?

WHAT IS GREATNESS IN LITERATURE?

It is a truism to state that the test of a work of literature is not to be found solely in its formal ideology. The most cursory examination of a few great works of literature will prove the validity of this truism.

Many of us recognize Tolstoy as a great writer, a genius, and a thinker of the first order. Is this because of the formal attitudes—the ideology—in his major works? In *Anna Karenina*, during the course of the novel, the character Levin develops the conception of political nonresistance which had become part of the gospel of Tolstoyism. Levin found reasons for refusing to take an interest in public affairs, and these reasons were Tolstoy's own for formulating this doctrine. Because we disagree with Tolstoy's views represented in his characterization of Levin, will we therefore deny the greatness of *Anna Karenina*? In *War and Peace* Tolstoy presents a view of history that succeeds in atomizing history to the degree that makes it impossible to distinguish between factors essential and of weight in the influencing of events and those incidental or secondary. According to this conception of history, every human being of a specific period influences the history of that period. History is the result of all the actions and all the thoughts of every human being. In a sense, this is correct. The history of man is everything that happens to man. But can we seek to explain and to understand man if we apply this conception concretely? If we do, we have no means of truly determining which factors are essential and important in a given historic study and which ones are nonessential. Not fully accepting this theory of history, which is imbedded in the very warp and woof of *War and Peace,* and which is also presented in the novel in essay form, do we therefore deny the value of this work?

Balzac was antidemocratic, and his formal attitudes were those prevailing at the time of the Restoration, which followed the fall of Napoleon. The formal view of Theodore Dreiser concerning man's place in the universe includes crude materialism and social Darwinism. Are his books, therefore, to be dismissed? Examples to demonstrate this point are endless. If we literally adopt such a view of literature, we thereby deny ourselves an appreciation of many of the greatest works of the past. We cannot then appreciate the literature and the art that preceded democracy, because it is not democratic. If we are socialists, we cannot appreciate the great literature of the modern age and, even more important, we will be incapable of explaining literature. If we demand that literature reflect in a direct, obvious, and mechanical fashion, the major struggles of the period from which it springs or with which it deals, what are we to say of such a novel as *Wuthering Heights?* This work—in my opinion one of the greatest of all English novels—describes characters who lived during the period when Bonaparte was at the height of his power. Withal, it has nothing to say of the danger of old "Bony" invading England. Is it therefore invalidated as a novel?

Literature is one of the arts which re-create the consciousness and the conscience of a period. It tells us what has happened to man, what could have happened to him, what man has imagined might happen to him. It presents the environments, the patterns of destiny, the joys and the sorrows, the tribulations, the dreams, the fantasies, the aspirations, the cruelties, the shames, the dreams, of men and women. Life is full of mysteries, and one of the major mysteries of life is man himself. Literature probes that mystery. Just as science helps man to understand nature, literature helps man to understand himself. Just as science makes human the forces of nature in the sense that it makes possible the construction of instruments for controlling these forces, so does literature aid in making man human to himself. Literature, by its very nature, cannot, in and of itself, solve social and political problems. Any solution of a social or political problem in a work of literature is a purely intellectual solution. These problems are problems of action. Every problem delimits the kind of means which can, and those which cannot, be of use in its solution. This statement applies in logic, in mathematics, in the physical sciences, in the solution of social and political problems, and in the problems that any artist must face in his own work. It is just as absurd to assume that you can solve political and social problems with a poem as it is to expect a painter, by painting a picture, to save from death a man stricken with appendicitis.

HOW MUCH LITERATURE CAN DO

Literature generally reflects life. It often limps, even crawls, behind events. This is especially so in periods of great social crisis and of historic convulsion. What is the great literary work of the Napoleonic period—one which parallels our own age? It is Stendhal's *The Red and the Black*. But Stendhal did not write this novel when he was with the French army in Moscow. He wrote it some time after the Battle of Waterloo.

Some of those who take a view of literature contrary to the one I am presenting here demand that the writer be a prophet. His duty is to foresee what is to come, not merely to reflect what has already come—including what man has already dreamed, imagined, constructed in his own head—as well as what has happened in the sense of actual objective events. Let us examine this view concretely. What is prophecy? It is prediction. Whether one makes a prophecy, or prediction, on the basis of an inner vision or as the result of a close scientific investigation, that prophecy, or prediction, proves nothing. It is merely a statement of probability. It must be validated by the occurrence of the events predicted. Besides, it is obvious that when one makes a prediction one should base that prediction on relevant evidence. Therefore I ask: Is a lyric poem the proper form in which to predict historic events? If so, why do we not elect lyric poets as our political leaders? It is the exercise of simple intelligence not to confuse problems. We do not ask our doctors, our dentists, our scientists, our politicians, or our mechanics to confuse problems; we ask only our poets and our novelists to do this.[4]

Furthermore, those who want to officialize literature—those who insist that the artist wear the uniform of an ideology—persist in calling writers who refuse to comply with their demand skeptics and cynics. Often they use the words "skeptic" and "cynic" as if they were synonymous. These words do not necessarily have the same meaning. A skeptic doubts. A cynic is without faith. It is possible to doubt, to be critical, and still to have faith. Moreover, there is no necessary opposition between skepticism and faith. Without a skepticism sufficient to enable us to be critical of evidence, we would have a faith that is unwarranted. We would then believe something without knowing why we believe it. Also, to say that a writer is skeptical or cynical does not necessarily constitute a valid ground for criticism. Was there no skepticism, no cynicism, in Shakespeare? Is there no skepticism in the Bible? Tolstoy was more than skeptical of modern capitalism and of the efficacy of political action; in addition, he was a pacifist. A pacifist is obvi-

[4] I have here discussed prophecy in literature in terms of the prediction of events. Those who demand that the poet play the role of prophet from a regressively cultural point of view base their contention on the traditional philosophical conception of cognition as the sole factor in the process of knowledge. They then assume that the insights and "intuitions" of the poet constitute a form of knowing superior to that embodied in scientific method. They want to substitute the poet for the political theorist and analyst and for the scientist. There is, however, a sense in which the poet—Shelley, for instance—plays a role that can be considered analogous to that of the prophet. When a poet or novelist emphasizes the need for a change in values and attitudes required by the demands of social evolution, his role then is more or less analogous to that of the prophet. However, to perform this role he must have more than an alleged superior form of knowing—which is assumed to be poetic insight.

ously skeptical of the social value of war. Generally speaking, it is the realistic writers who are called skeptical and cynical. Those who make this charge against realists do not, however, examine what the realistic writer has to say. They don't examine the conditions that he describes. In many instances the realist describes injustice, misery, spiritual poverty, and material poverty. The world described by modern realists is not free from the conditions producing these results. No less a person than the President of the United States, President Roosevelt, has spoken of "one third of a nation" submerged in poverty, suffering from all the physical and mental ills bred by poverty. But if the realistic novelist deals with existing conditions, if he dares to re-create a true and revealing picture of these conditions, of the patterns of destiny of the characters who are educated and live under such conditions, he is a skeptic and a cynic. The attempt to tell the truth in a precise, concrete, and uncompromising manner is demoralizing. And what is the proposed alternative to this type of literature? It is: The advice to write about justice, about morality, about heroism, and about greatness in general—that is, in the abstract. Just to state many of these arguments is sufficient. It even becomes embarrassing to be forced to answer them in detail.

THE ROLE OF THE WRITER

He who would put literature in uniform is afraid of literature, and his fear of literature reveals a more fundamental fear—that of social change. The demand that literature conform comes from fear, not from confidence and not from faith. Literature in the modern world could not thrive under official control. The result of official control would be silencing, crushing, destroying, the really talented among our writers and so enable those who are not serious, those who are not truly talented, those who have nothing to say, to come to the front. The notion that the serious literary artist is a major element in demoralizing a society is absurd on its face. No society can be demoralized with a few books. If a society is demoralized, the reasons for that condition go much deeper than the circulation of a few books. The actual spy, the actual saboteur, the actual agent of enemy governments, and so on, do not have the time—nor do they usually have the sensibility, the imagination, the intelligence, the culture, or the background—to create a work of literature. He who makes such charges against the artist makes them because he dare not look conditions in the face. And to look conditions in the face is precisely what the serious writer tries to do. In some instances these conditions exist in society at large; in other instances these conditions are in the mind, in the emotions, in the dreams, and in the consciousness of the artist himself. In all serious literature there is truth—truth of insight, of observation, truth about the social relationships of the world, as well as truth about the consciousness of men. And the truth will make men free, although it may disturb the critical legislator and the ideological smuggler.

It is inept, absurd, downright silly, to argue that in a world torn by the greatest convulsions of the modern period, literature can hide away in a hothouse. I make no such claims. I am not demanding here that literature exist in any ivory tower. What I do stress, however, is that literature must solve its own problems and that it cannot be turned into the mere handmaiden of politics and into a mere looking-glass of ideologies. The justification of literature must be made in terms of the functions it performs and not by seeking to make it perform functions for which it is unfitted. When Ralph Waldo Emerson died, William James, who as a boy had known Emerson, wrote that although Emerson was a monist—James himself defended a conception of an open, pluralistic universe—Emerson did not suppress facts in order to substantiate his monism. This statement provides us with the formula for understanding and tolerance, in both the world of ideas and the world of art. If the writer has not suppressed the facts, we can seek to understand him; and if we find value in his work, we can justify that work despite agreement or disagreement with his formal ideas. And it is to be remembered that in art the facts are not statistical; the facts are perceptions, observations, insights, revelations of certain aspects of those mysteries of life which surround us on every side and which exist even in our own consciousness.

It is now almost three centuries to the year since John Milton wrote his *Areopagitica*, one of the most eloquent defenses of freedom of inquiry and freedom for the artist that has ever been written. Milton wrote: "As good almost . . . kill a man as kill a good book: who kills a man kills a reasonable creature . . . but he who destroys a good book kills reason itself." What Milton said is in the spirit of the eloquent apology of Socrates when he stood on trial for his life—charged with having demoralized the youth of Athens—and when he declared to his judges: ". . . the unexamined life is not worth living. . . ." And, to conclude, serious literature is one of the most powerful means contrived by the human spirit for examining life. This in itself is the basic justification of literature in any period. This is the answer that the artist can confidently hurl back at all Philistines who fear to permit the examination of life.

1942

The Faith of Lewis Mumford[1]

> *"In a time of faith, skepticism is the most intolerable of insults."*—RANDOLPH BOURNE

I

THE SECOND WORLD WAR has produced a new generation of American war intellectuals who so resemble their predecessors of the First World War that differences are scarcely discernible. Go to the library and read the articles in the dusty magazines of 1917 and 1918; glance through the now-forgotten books of that period. And then consider what contemporary intellectuals are saying in the press and what they are writing in the magazines, the liberal journals, and the books they dash off with such fevered haste. The war intellectuals of today seem almost to be plagiarizing their predecessors. All the arguments

[1] Since this essay was written in the autumn of 1940, Mr. Mumford has published *The Condition of Man,* the third volume of the series begun in *Technics and Civilization* and *The Culture of the Cities.* I had proposed to review this book at length, but after having read half of it carefully, I realized that there was nothing essential to say of Mr. Mumford's work that I had not stated in this essay. I then skimmed through the rest of it. As was to be expected, this book was hailed by popular reviewers and others as another major contribution to knowledge. But it is characterized by the same fuzziness, obscuranticism, mixture of the grandiose and the trivial, as one notes in practically all of Mr. Mumford's writing. The introduction opens as follows: "What is man? What meaning has his life? What is his origin, his condition, his destiny?" Mr. Mumford has risen to nothing less than the posing of these questions. But his answers are no different, in essence, than those provided in his other books. Rebuilding of self, renewal, "organicism." "Today our best plans miscarry because they are in the hands of people who have undergone no inner growth. Most of those people have shrunk from facing the world crisis and they have no notion of the manner in which they themselves have helped to bring it

and slogans echo those of 1917. New actors are performing old and familiar roles.[2]

If there are differences between the two generations of war intellectuals, the major mark of distinction is to be found in the fact that the contemporary generation is more reactionary than that of 1917. Struggling to express a faith to justify a new war in defense of democracy, many contemporary intellectuals have already turned their backs on what is best in the democratic

---

about . . . They are in a power dive and their controls have frozen. By closing their eyes they think they can avoid a crash." Is Mr. Mumford *serious*? If so, let him say this and much more in the most explicit and unambiguous terms to Mr. Roosevelt, to Mr. Churchill, and to Marshal Stalin. Mr. Mumford continues his course of misunderstanding Marxism and socialism, along with other of his misunderstandings. For instance: "And in the great successful personalities of the communist movement, Marx's aggressive and domineering impulses played a disproportionate part and rippled on through their followers. Abraham Lincoln in his charity, his humility, and his self-criticism, was a far better incarnation of the spirit of socialism." To the melodramatic and unhistorical notion of the "Baroque" capitalist he adds the aggressive and uncharitable notion of the immoral socialist or communist, and he cites Stalin's pact with Hitler as a fruit of Marxism. He makes no attempt to show whether or not this pact was consistent with the ideas of Marx and Lenin; it is a historic fact that Trotsky condemned this pact. Further on, Mussolini, a renegade from socialism, is cited as having reaped the "full harvest of practical Marxism." All this, and on top of it Abraham Lincoln as the "incarnation of the spirit of socialism." It is no disrespect to Lincoln to say that *he was not a socialist*. He wasn't. In a message to Congress, Lincoln once said: "Capital is only the fruit of labor." But "Capital has its rights, which are as worthy of protection as any other rights." And he said that the relationship between capital and labor produced "mutual benefits." Mumford's humanitarianism is vague and Utopian. Utopianism in 1944, at that! Mumford on socialism is no different from Mumford on anything else. At another place in his latest opus, he says, "Only the acceptance of a mystery beyond the compass of reason keeps man's life from becoming devaluated and his spirit from becoming discouraged over the reports of reason." No, a mystery is a problem to be conquered by reason. Further on: "Freud was an unwilling Augustinian." And the Papacy "has proved the most successful form of government in human history." In general, Mumford's organicism continues to be what I have described it as in this essay.

[2] By now, the spectacle they have made of themselves is dismal beyond words. Events sweep over them like tides, and they grow increasingly anxious and disturbed. Their writings, on the whole, read like a fever chart. Every time they hail events as a new victory for their views they sink into fresh doldrums. The formula of their writings is practically as follows:—*we are winning! we are sinking.*

tradition. Asking us to defend this tradition arms in hand, they themselves are overthrowing it. A veritable cult of the irrational has grown up among them. Today they not only denounce Adolf Hitler: many of them also condemn what is best in the modern tradition of reason and science. In its place they would substitute the values of a feudal past. Literally, they would have us die in the defense of the ideals of the eleventh and twelfth centuries.

Lewis Mumford is one of the leading spokesmen of the new cult of the irrational, and his books, *Men Must Act* and *Faith for Living*, can be accepted as its next.

In this article I shall not only examine these two works; I shall also consider Lewis Mumford's past and some of the sources of his inspiration. In the past Lewis Mumford was a reformist. He believed that social progress could be attained by an adaptation to capitalist society rather than by overthrowing it. And he stated that the power state, based on force and class oppression, was being gradually rendered obsolete, and that in its place, the service state has already come into being.[3] An admirer of Randolph Bourne, he condemned the First World War, after it was over, adopted a liberal, pacifist position, and proclaimed that if America entered another imperialist war, his duty as a writer would be to do all in his power to prevent a military dictatorship from imposing fascism on America. While he was anti-fascist, he failed to take German fascism seriously less than a year before Hitler came to power. He heralded the new age of reason, science and justice; he even predicted that the first signs of this age were plainly apparent in modern society. He wrote the programs of this new age, but was consistently vague concerning the means for its attainment. In a quixotic manner he skipped over the central question of state and class power. His views, partially derived from traditional reaction, were based mainly on a defective conception of society.

Today, he stands as an example of the bankruptcy of reform-

[3] In *The Condition of Man,* he is fearful that "the capitalist dog has returned to his old vomit," and in order to go forward, we must have "stabilized personalities," etc.

ism. Instead of the new order, the world is torn apart in a bitter war. His predictions and prophecies have not been fulfilled. That which he did not expect to happen, happened: fascism triumphed in many European countries. Now the anti-fascist war leaves men like Mumford as uneasy as ever. In such circumstances, Lewis Mumford falls back on those sources that have always nourished him. He brings into the open the reactionary implications that were always latent in his writing. And, simultaneously, he bitterly denounces other intellectuals as passive aids of Hitlerism because, he charges, they did not take fascism seriously.

II

Lewis Mumford's master has been Patrick Geddes, a town planner, nature lover, an educator, a man of good will, and sponsor of "the scientific doctrine of civism." Geddes styled himself an "ideopraxist," that is, a practical idealist. He acknowledged his intellectual debt to nineteenth-century French feudal thinkers; in fact, he defended De Maistre, De Bonald, and Le Play from the charge of being reactionary. In essence a reformist, he had grandiose dreams of a new age of regional culture, beautiful cities, and a happy humanity, which, he argued, would pay dividends to the capitalists and to society as a whole. This new age was more than a dream to him, for he saw concrete proofs of it in the life of his time. Mumford and Geddes have dreamed the same dreams.

In 1915, when Europe was being torn apart in a bloody carnage, Patrick Geddes, in *Cities in Evolution,* wrote about "the nobler cities of a not necessarily distant future" and proclaimed "the neotechnic order so plainly arising in other lands—Norway being the best example, as having no paleotechnic development." He found real evidence of the new era, "Eutopia," in the Kaiser's Germany. Mumford saw the same "Eutopia" in the Germany of the Weimar Republic.

Lewis Mumford was in Germany in 1932, precisely at the time when Germany was being split asunder by the threat of civil war. During this period the Nazis were invading working-

class districts of German cities and there were frequent week-
end riots. National Socialism was already in power in Prussia
and Thuringia. The Weimar Republic was a vanishing shadow,
which Brüning's decree laws had been unable to save. Germany's
reformist holiday was over. Returning to America, Mumford
wrote an article, "Notes on Germany," for *The New Republic*
(October 26, 1932). What did he see in the Germany of 1932?
He discovered that the German people were enjoying excellent health and that "the cult of the sun was the symbol of an
almost religious revival that had taken place in Germany since
the war." He lauded the civic improvement and the growth of
interest in sports and physical culture. Even a National Socialist
had, in his pre-Nazi days, written a book about naked women
that "gave a deep impulse both to the culture of the body and
its comely development." He stated that "the new Germany"
had "utilized all the latent good of the old Germany."

To be sure, there was a black side to the picture. Over-
expansion had created a false boom.[4] This had produced an
inevitable depression. There was profiteering. Large corporation heads had voted themselves salaries that were abnormally
large, even for capitalism. And the workers had become "uppity." They had built ostentatious headquarters that violated
the canons of functionalism.

These and other instances of bad foresight notwithstanding,
he was convinced that Germany had made immeasurably
greater investments in life-giving activities and community
welfare than had America during the immediately preceding

4 Mumford has never understood the function performed by credit in a capitalist
economy. He does not seem to understand that credit is essential for business
expansion, and that business expansion is necessary for capitalist economy, and,
further, that business expansion will inevitably become overexpanded. Consequently, there must be inflation of credit. Not grasping the real function of
credit, his denunciations of speculation generally remain on a purely moralistic
level: What he sees thus as the lamentable mistake of the past is, *in reality,*
an absolute necessity of capitalist economy. In *The Condition of Man* he discusses expansion and says that unless a balanced economy is established there
must be an expansion by war or stabilization through monopoly. A new
ideology is therefore necessary in order to create a post-capitalist economy.
But before these changes can be established, "the inner crisis in our civilization
must be resolved . . ."

period of world prosperity. Germany had invested in works
of enduring social and human value, such as fine buildings,
model homes, civic improvements of various kinds whereas
America, in the same period, had mainly manufactured too
many gadgets, fixtures, automobiles, and shell-like suburban
homes. "Germany is in fact perhaps the one country in Europe
that would be capable of instituting a complete communistic
society without altering many of its fundamental attitudes and
without being terribly impeded by the weakness of the old
order." Also: "Order, authority, technical ability and personal
initiative are all present together in Germany, and thanks to
the social influence of the impoverished small nobility and the
professors, pecuniary standards have never been solely dominant." Thus Mumford met the future in the Germany of 1932.

And the Nazis? Of course, they were reactionaries. But
"Hitler's notions of dictatorship were but the maggots actively
appropriating the dead flesh of the dynastic system." Hitler
was tied to the old order, which Mumford believed could not
seriously impede progress. In fact, Weimar Germany was using
the latent good of the old order. Hence, what were a few
maggots, when you could see the future in the short skirts,
the real sun-tan, and the hockey shin-guards on the brown
legs of a German burgher housewife as she rode on a Sunday
streetcar to the athletic field? For such was one of the signs
of hope he emphasized. He concluded this article with "Whenever I was a little upset by the blatant childishness and insanity
of the middle class Nazis, I would think of the decent and self-
respecting German worker, patient, methodical, perhaps a little
stupid, but always honest; and I would be reassured. At the
bottom, in Germany, there is sanity and strength." [5]

In the Germany of 1932, the momentous question of the

[5] In *The Condition of Man* Mumford tells us that "Spengler's Downfall" was
an image of fascist states to come and that "He who understood the significance
of Spengler's art of prophecy had little to learn from the further course of
Europe's history." Mumford had read Spengler before 1932. From this it is clear
that Mumford meets with great difficulty in learning; he even finds it difficult
to learn after the facts have happened. This defines his value as a prophet quite
demonstratively.

hour was not nude sun-bathing; it was—*state power.* Something, apparently, had happened to the "impoverished small nobility" and to "the professors." Adolph Hitler came to power early in 1933; the rest is modern history.

Today, Lewis Mumford damns scores of his fellow men with the accusation that they never took fascism seriously. Van Wyck Brooks, Waldo Frank, and many others believe these accusations. From *Men Must Act,* we learn: "Out of the spinelessness of 'liberalism' the backbone of fascism has been created." In *Faith for Living,* Mumford wrote: "There is plenty of evidence at hand to prove that the liberal, face to face with fascism, can literally not find words to condemn it. This refusal to recognize evil as evil has fatally delayed the world's reaction against barbarism." Also: "The incurable tendency of the liberal is to believe the best about everybody . . . continued practice [of "this virtue"] . . . is . . . a treasonable act . . ."

In *Men Must Act* and *Faith for Living* Mr. Mumford also discusses the German people and German tradition. For instance, in *Faith for Living,* he wrote: "The people who turn their heads away when a Brown Shirt kicks a helpless old man . . . the people who cower behind their doors when . . . the Gestapo rouses some poor victim at midnight . . . are passive supporters of fascism." Although he once discovered "personal initiative" in Germany, he now tells us that "Fascism has happened . . . in . . . Germany" because of that nation's lack of a "long tradition of freedom." As a matter of fact, "only a handful of German thinkers have ever had even a glimmer of the meaning of freedom." Despite what he said in 1932, of the old order in Germany, he now tells us that "The fundamental ideology of fascism was first formulated in the sermons, letters and exhortations of Martin Luther." In *The Condition of Man,* Luther is an earlier "isolationist." And this ideology has persisted in German thought from the Reformation to Adolf Hitler.[6]

---

6 Mumford has drawn heavily from German sources. The long bibliographies appended both to *Technics and Civilization* and *The Culture of the Cities*

Unfairly equating Marxism and Stalinism, Mumford now claims that the Marxists failed to understand fascism because they see ideas merely as the shadow of economics (a gross simplification of the Marxian conception of ideology). To him, this explains why the Marxists made "their ludicrous errors" in meeting this "new force" which is as old as Martin Luther. They did not understand that in relation to fascism, economics is the expression of "far more subjective politics." However, precisely during the time that Lewis Mumford was evaluating the social significance of short skirts and the cult of the sun in Germany, a Marxist named Leon Trotsky wrote *Germany, What Next?*, an urgent alarm-call for immediate and organized resistance to the Nazis. Trotsky said, "The [Italian] Fascist Government has maintained itself for ten years already. How much longer will it hold on? Without venturing into the risky business of setting dates, one can still say with assurance that Hitler's victory in Germany means a new and long lease of life for Mussolini. Hitler's crash will mean the beginning of the end for Mussolini." [7] Trotsky also sharply attacked the German Social Democrats for thinking fascism was merely a "crisis psychosis." Realizing that Hitler's ideas were far more sinister than any "maggots" eating the dead flesh of Hohenzollernism could ever be, Trotsky also wrote: "It is precisely the strength of Fascism and its onset that eliminate . . . the possibility of eschewing battle. Battle will have to be given."

Irony! Patrick Geddes *years ago* thought that the post-war generation of German burghers might find "a formative answer to the sphinx-riddle of politics." It has! And Lewis Mumford now puzzles over that riddle.

---

include a number of German works. In many respects he is an Americanized version of Spengler, whom he now condemns. He and Spengler both think in the same far-fetched manner of analogy. I think the reader should remember this now when Mumford has revised his judgments on German thought.

[7] In *Men Must Act* Mumford states: "In 1928 it was still possible to treat fascism lightly: Mussolini's operatic gestures were rather a caricature of power than a display of it."

III

When there was much talk of war in June, 1935—as there was during the entire post-Versailles period of "peace"—Lewis Mumford contributed to a symposium on war conducted by the magazine, *The Modern Quarterly*. To the question "What will you do when America goes to war?" Mumford answered in part, "In general, I oppose war because of its imbecility, its absence of human purpose, its brutalization of life, its abject failure to achieve reasonable goods, and *its futile simplification of all the conflicts and real issues involved in life in communities.* . . . But I am no absolute pacifist [???]; it is neither the waste of war nor its toll of death that appalls me, but the fact that this waste and these deaths come to no purpose, by reason of the very technique of fighting and its special be-haviour pattern—*no matter how just and rational the cause seems at the outset. War is always a losing fight even when it is a just one.*" (Italics, mine.) In the event of war, he declared that "his duty as a writer" would be "to remain sane, to think clearly, *to correct emotional distortions* and patriotic biases, and *in general see to it that the fight did not lead to . . . the patriotic setting up of a permanent military political organiza-tion, namely Fascism.*" (Again, my italics.)

Lewis Mumford's *The Culture of the Cities* (published in 1938) states: "Only in times of war . . . when a pervading sense of fear sanctions the extirpation of differences, does the national state conform to its ideal pattern. All the great national states, and the empires formed around a national core, are at bottom war-states; their politics is war-politics; and the all absorbing preoccupation of its governing classes lies in collec-tive preparation for armed assault. The final caricature of this tendency is National Socialist Germany today . . ." He divided the "great national states" into two groups, those of the past —the United States, Great Britain, France and Russia—and those of the present—Germany, Italy and Japan. Mumford here spoke the language of the Popular Front, of which the Stalinists formed the backbone.[8] *Men Must Act* (published in 1939) also retained some of the illusions spread by the Popular Front. Speaking of Munich, he said, "The dangers [of war] were exaggerated by the politicians of England and France—and Hitler's prospects of an imminent and early defeat were deliberately withheld from view—in order to make easy the contemplated surrender." In other words, he followed the liberals he now condemns, in underestimating the military strength of Germany as late as 1939. He even declared, "In propagandist warfare only fascists are capable of invading the enemy with airplanes." Immersed in the ideology of the Popular Front, he disregarded the warnings of anti-Stalinists who forecast a rapprochement between Germany and Russia. He still condemns this part as immoral, but treats it as a consequence, among other things, of Marx's aggressive personality. But in 1940, he discovered that Russia was the first fascist state. His disdain for the liberal intellectuals who were duped by the Stalinist Popular Front ill befits the man.

In 1940 he spoke in terms of holy crusades. He was prepared to abrogate civil liberties at home as a means of destroying fascism abroad. Those who opposed American entry into this war were cowardly—fearful of losing their own miserable lives. In *Men Must Act* he told us that in order "To make their tacit alliance with fascism easier, the absolute pacifists have, until recently, adopted an optimistic attitude toward fascism itself." From *Faith for Living*, we learn that "To regard all this violence" of war and fascism "as primarily the symptom of economic maladjustment is a perversion of good sense." It is all the product of a "metaphysical state of mind." Today, 1944, he writes: "On capitalist terms there is no 'moral equivalent of war.' That was the illusion that should have been burned forever by the calamitous depression that started in 1929."

[8] In *The Culture of the Cities* Mumford wrote concerning the role of Protestantism in the break-up of the Middle Ages: "Cleavages in matters of faith increased the forces of economic disruption and further destroyed the possibilities of creating a *united front*." (My italics.) In a sense he even read the Popular Front backward into history. He now uses isolationism in the same *ex post facto* manner.

Here we have, in part, the political anatomy of Lewis Mumford.

IV

Lewis Mumford's faith in the organic is unshakable. What are the major sources and features of his concept of the organic?

A basic source of this concept is the Catholic idea of the unity of society in God. He derives this inspiration from De Maistre and De Bonald, via Patrick Geddes and Victor Branford. De Maistre and De Bonald were the masters of counter-revolutionary thought (against democracy and the Great French Revolution) in nineteenth-century France. They defended the ideal of a feudal society. Rejecting the theory of the social contract, they offered the alternative explanation that society is the product of the fatherhood of God; De Maistre insisted that, in the literal sense of the word, kings were appointed by God. He considered man-made laws and written constitutions defective; man by himself can invent nothing that is productive of salutary consequences. Good laws are the inspiration of God—and the king declares these laws. Eighteenth-century individualism, the "cause" of the French Revolution, is an example of the evil man produces when he takes onto his own shoulders those responsibilities and functions that truly belong to God.[9] Mere knowledge will endanger society. De Bonald said that "the result of increasing knowledge was the desire for domination"; De Maistre envisaged the ruin of any society that substituted science for religion as the basis of education. To them, medieval society throughout the Holy Roman Empire was built on a religion unifying society with God. Hence, it was organic. This is an argument by analogy, comparing society to the human body. Just as in the human body the various members are functional to one another, so is it in organic society. God is the head of such a society, and his representatives are the Pope and the

[9] De Bonald once declared that when God wanted to punish the French nation he took the Bourbons away from it. Needless to say, this would make the Jacobins agents of the Almighty, and the guillotine would be the hand of God.

monarch. The various classes are the members or parts of the social organism. The relationship of the various classes to the head are analogous to the relationship of the head to, say, the stomach and the limbs. The supervening institution that co-ordinates this functional relationship—the soul of the organism—is the Church. Through it, the functions of the members are established, one to the other. Concretely, this means that the classes need one another: the noble needs the peasant, and the peasant the noble. Each owes obligations to the other. These obligations are laid down by the Church and expressed in the juridical relationships of feudal law and in the common practices of feudal customs. They produce a set of ethical values. Class antagonisms and struggles violate these values and endanger the organism. Social harmony is produced by class stratification. Here is a hierarchical view of society based on the productive relationships prevalent in the Middle Ages.

While De Maistre and De Bonald were men of intelligence, the entire current of modern history was opposed to their ideas. Hence they exist as purely literary figures. Their views are antibourgeois, and they helped give rise to feudal conceptions for the reform of society—feudal socialism. Of this, Marx and Engels wrote, "The aristocracy, in order to rally the people to them, waved the proletarian alms-bag in front for a banner. But the people, as often as it joined them, saw on their hindquarters the old feudal coats-of-arms, and deserted with loud and irreverent laughter."

Le Play, a mining engineer, sociologist, and Senator during the Empire of Napoleon III, was one of the continuators of the tradition of De Maistre and De Bonald, both of whom he often cited approvingly. Le Play had been seriously frightened by the libertarian revolutions that shook France at the end of the eighteenth century and during the nineteenth. After 1871, he defended Napoleon III from the accusation of having engineered the disasters that befell France; these he laid at the foot of the Paris Commune. The major aim of Le Play was that of securing *le paix sociale*. He made elaborate case studies of highly selected types of European working-class families, which he cited to prove that society could prosper only when it was based on the observance of ancient usages of custom and on the Ten Commandments. His idea of the relationship between employer and worker rested on the feudal conceptions of hierarchy and mutual obligations. He saw the family as a miniature of the State and considered patriarchal society as the type best fitted for the ideal society. Le Play urged that the family be rooted in the place. The family hearth, firmly situated in the place, helped to create a better barrier against forces and ideas tending to disintegrate the family. In addition, he proposed a close relationship between factory and family, obviously modelled on the feudal connection between noble and serf. One of the benefits of such a connection, he contended, would be that the father and son could prosper on small wages because the children, the mother, and the old people could obtain gainful work in proportion to their capabilities. In a society organized along the lines which Le Play outlined, a central role for the maintenance of the harmony and the preservation of tradition was left to what he termed the Social Authorities. These were the best men of the community—persons of probity, high morals and disinterested community spirit—who would serve as models of conduct and guiding intelligence. By necessity, they would have to belong to the upper classes. Also, he urged employers to accept as a duty the provision of at least subsistence wages to their workers during bad times. For unless the employer did make such provisions, the workers would be likely to listen to agitators, who were democratic, or even worse. He did not visualize the workers as an independent or decisive factor in society. Therefore he did not blame the workers or the lower classes in general for the revolutions of nineteenth-century France. The germ of revolution was in the French nation as a whole. The evil influence of Jean Jacques Rousseau and the corruption of the upper classes had stimulated these calamitous uprisings. Le Play can be summarized by this statement: He applied to the workers the notion that if one throws a few bones to a dog, the dog won't bite people. His views and criticism were aristocratic. He "waved the proletarian alms-bag."

To the conception of the organic, which comes from Catholic sources, Patrick Geddes added two ideas: evolution and vitalism. These are wedded to each other in a crude edition of Bergson's theory of creative evolution.[10] Geddes and his collaborator, J. A. Thompson, describe *an organic philosophy of nature* in their little book, *Biology*. To them, biology was the science which would unify all other sciences, and they provided a transformation formula which was supposed to outline the means for achieving this unification: organism is the function of environment; environment is the function of organism. They attributed to nature the characteristics of the human biological organism, and believed that "there must be throughout nature something of that psychic light which even in man is still but approaching the perfect day." Evolutionary and vitalistic ideas permitted Geddes to see not only society but also nature, the entire world, as *organic*. A secularized interpretation of ideas concerning the mystical body of Christ is rendered evolutionary through dependence on Darwinism. It becomes creative and progressive with the aid of both Darwinism and vitalism. Man, society, and nature are unified. Mumford has taken over these views. He tells us in *Technics and Civilization* that "the very distribution of the elements on the earth's crust, their quantity, their solubility, their specific gravity, their distribution and chemical combinations, are life-furthering and life-sustaining. Even the most rigorous scientific description of the physical basis of life indicates it to be internally teleological." Mumford is a shallow vitalist.[11] And in *Faith for Living* he draws the

10 In *The Condition of Man* Mumford declares that among modern philosophers, Bergson, along with Emerson, comes closest to Jesus, who was "organic," a "mystic and a psychologist." Perhaps one might write an essay—"The Gospels and élan vital."

11 Once we understand Mumford's "organic" mysticism, certain aspects of his writing are no longer confusing. His animism, for example. He tends to see the machine in terms of an analogy with the animal organism. This explains why he calls some machines organic and others inorganic. To him, the clock and the railroad are inorganic; contraceptives are organic. In general, the visible is usually inorganic and the invisible organic. Also, we see the sources of his style. His images often tend to be of two kinds: (1) analogies to the biological organism, which on one hand relate to health or on the other refer to decay, disease, and death; (2) analogies to the processes of vegetation.

complete circle of an Emersonian oversoul around his universe:
"Men are individually nothing except in relation to that greater
reality, Man. And Man himself is nought except in relation
to that greater reality which he calls divine. Thought, art, love
are all intimations of this divinity, flickerings of man-made
filaments that connect, in our imaginations, with distant flashes
in the dark impenetrable sky." As he says in *The Condition of
Man*, man's destiny gives, *perhaps* to the cosmos, "an emergent
end."

Keeping in mind these factors in the background of Mumford's views of the *organic*, we can now examine the function
these views perform. Geddes and Mumford have both written
in Protestant countries, and their appeals have been addressed
to many Protestants whose ideas come from the Enlightenment.
Liberal and socialist ideas of reform made much more headway
in the last century than did those of feudal thinkers. Geddes
and Mumford could not present the ideas of De Maistre and
De Bonald precisely in their original form. But the imprint of
these ideas, nonetheless, is stamped on Mumford's work. We can
see these ideas in Mumford's "organic" and schematized interpretation of history. Medieval society was organic society. In
the post-medieval period it has been inorganic. Social unity
was destroyed. Fragments of medieval culture have persisted
in this inorganic period, and that constitutes the main source of
tradition. Since the eighteenth century, in particular, these fragments have tended to disappear at an accelerated pace. In recent
years, roughly, since 1870, and more noticeably since the lifetime of Patrick Geddes, there have been signs and developments
indicating that society is entering a new organic period, one
that is on a higher level than the organic period of the Middle
Ages.[12] Geddes saw signs of the new organic society in Norway,

[12] Mumford, in *The Golden Day,* and Frank, in *The Rediscovery of America,*
extended this schematization by applying it to America. The New England
"Golden Day" thus becomes a kind of Middle Ages. The Gilded Age, "the
brown decades," becomes the inorganic period. The task of the rediscovery
of America is that of creating the new synthesis, establishing a new "Golden
Day" on a higher level. Mumford's fondness for the sentimental tautology,
a "usable past," grows out of this schematization. The same kind of pattern of

in Burgher Germany, and in the First World War. Mumford has seen these signs in the "robust political life" that flourished a few years ago in Sunnyside, Long Island, in the philosophy of Alfred North Whitehead, in the present status of biological science, and elsewhere. In Geddes' time, the new "integration" had reached the point where the doctrines of both revolution and reaction were "ageing." In Mumford's time, the new "synthesis" as we have already seen, developed to a very advanced point in Germany, by 1932. Although Hitler destroyed the continued progress of the new synthesis in Germany, integration continued on the march through the pages of *Technics and Civilization* and *The Culture of the Cities*. The new integration is today a bit more precarious than it was a few years ago. But if we all strive to become the "new type" of "stabilized" personality, everything is again possible. We can set the new integration marching.

Applying his view of the "organic," Mumford idealizes the Middle Ages. His interpretation of history is sentimental. He makes arbitrary judgments of good and bad, using the "organic" as a criterion of evaluation. Thus he distorts his romantic view of the Middle Ages and applies it to substantiate his dispraise of the entire post-medieval period down to the time of the "new integration." Whereas he tends to deduce the character of the Middle Ages from the ideas of unity and harmony of that time, he tends to see the ideas of post-medieval times in terms of a crude correlation between the practices of capitalism and a melodramatic idea of the ravenous capitalist. Today we learn from *The Condition of Man* there is a type worse than the capitalist—the "isolationist." Compared to the latter, "the working beliefs of the imperialist and the international financier had actual moral superiority, for at their brutal worst, the latter had at least been interested enough in their remote brothers to, wish to exploit them. This low, negative sense of human solidarity was more defensible than the notion

---

"organic" and "inorganic" is introduced in *The Condition of Man*. This time it is focused as the rational and irrational. Greece declined, for instance, because it did not synthesize these in a higher "organicism."

a country could at will cut itself off from the rest of the human race, to its own profit and pride, as the . . . isolationists . . . advocated." Can muddle-headedness go further? He correlates isolationists of the present, fascists, nationalists of the past, Martin Luther, and others. The fact that in some instances the isolationists were also imperialists, the fact that nationalism has had different meanings in different periods— in brief, the facts of history are no trouble here.

But to continue, all forms of society have an organic character in consonance with the mode of productive relations prevalent in each society. The sentiment of unity prevalent in the Middle Ages and the harmony obtained in the functional relationships of the feudal order were based on class stratification, and these are in no sense to be lauded because there has been oppression under capitalism. Also, while class warfare under a capitalist mode of society has been fierce and bitter, this does not alter the fact that the Middle Ages were also rife with class struggle. Finally, just as the philosophies of both political democracy and socialism have assimilated the best of Christian ethics, so has modern science used, and developed out of, the thought of the Middle Ages. Mumford's interpretation of history is a fantasia. It is based on unwarranted analogies on the order of Spengler's, and it breaks the streams of historic continuity.

Mumford's conception of society as an organism provides the rationale for his ideas of social reform. Social problems are viewed as analogous to physical and/or mental illness. A social disease is the result of the mal-functioning of a member. If a part is out of gear, the whole is affected. The classes and social groups are all functions of one another.[13] Any function that is

[13] This explains why Mumford's thinking has led him so close to contemporary Catholic thinkers, who favor the corporate state, as well as to contemporary totalitarian thinkers. The idea of the corporate state of the Papal encyclicals is, and must be, based on the hypothesis that society is an organism. The corporations then represent the various members of the organism: they are functions of one another. Mumford is also close to the Austrian economist, Othmar Spann, who has helped break the ideological ground for fascism. His system of "universalism" is totalitarianism. He conceives society as an organism. The society that fits best into his system is that of the Middle Ages; it is his ideal society. Like Mumford, Spann criticizes bourgeois economists for having atomized

working anarchistically is destroying social integration. It focuses the problem of integration. The concept of the reform flowing from these assumptions is that of adaptation. Adaptation is the typical reformist's concept of social change. Society, the social and economic structure of society, is given. There must be adaptation to that which is given. The same concept can be described by the word *reintegration*. The ailing member must be restored to its proper function in the organism. The split-off part must again be put back into the whole. Thus is social harmony attained. The functional conception of society is substituted for the class conception. The asumption that society is an organism removes the hypothesis of economic determinism from its central position as a primary premise in the analysis of history and of social problems. Instead of looking on society as a structure organized in terms of productive relationships and economic interests, you see society as a whole. The community has precedence over the class. Here we have a secularized modern version of De Maistre's ideal of the harmonious society: in place of God, vague ethical notions are substituted.

Now, Mumford goes a step further in confusion. Now, we must begin making ourselves "organic" in order to make society "organic." And this means we must "think" like Mumford.

This spirit pervades Mumford's ideas of social reforms. He has postulated a "system" termed "basic communism." "A normalized mode of consumption is the basis of a rationalized mode of production," he says in *Technics and Civilization*. "Basic Communism" proposes a normalized basis of consumption for the entire community, which would set the groundwork for the planning of production. Thus does he offer a solu-

---

economics. He substitutes the conception of functions for that of causal relationships. Like Mumford, he stresses the necessity of seeing events and phenomena as qualities rather than as quantities, as if these categories were strictly polar opposites. In his system of universalism, he establishes a hierarchy of functions; Mumford implicitly also has the idea of a hierarchy of functions as the means for distributing consumer goods and for organizing the flow of social energies. For a while Spann was in favor with the Nazis and was invited to Berlin not long after Hitler came to power. However, he fell into disfavor.

tion for the problems generated by the functioning of capitalist economy—scarcity, unemployment, crises. The fundamental problem posed by a capitalist economy is seen as that of establishing a higher standard of consumption rather than one concerning a change in ownership of the means of production. "The problem presses for solution; but in one sense it has already been solved." How? For almost a century, widows, orphans, and others have been living well from insurance payments and stock dividends. This *rentier* class has produced "a Milton, a Shelley, a Darwin, a Ruskin . . ." If this plan is extended to the whole of society, so that all become one *rentier* class, the problem will be solved by the productive system. Society will pay everyone a kind of alimony. A basic income will be normalized. Production will be planned to satisfy the wants purchasable with this income. Competition for more goods will be centered around getting more than is procurable with the basic income. Thus will end the deadly "peaceful warfare" of competition. Everyone will be integrated into the harmonious community. Mumford does not specify how this plan is to be put into operation but says that it would be a tremendous human gain if it were.

He still emphasizes consumption, but has some modifications of his prescription in *The Condition of Man*. Thus: "Industry's market now depends upon a steady rise in the annual income of the worker. This vertical increase in consumption cannot be achieved by the nineteenth-century method of adding to the area of the market and the number of consumers. Rather, there must be a shift in capital investments from industries promising high profits to industries promising a better fulfillment of social need: a shift in expenditure from the luxury-stimulating industries to the life-maintaining industries: above all, there must be a shift in the standard of living, from one expressed in money rewards to one expressed in terms of direct biological, social and personal satisfactions . . . security is possible only in a stable economy." This has not been attained because leaders tried to maintain the system of the past. "Stabilization cannot be achieved by private initiative, even when its agents are great corporations and great trade unions: it demands a radical change in public policy, which must be argued before an electorate and decided by the democratic process, so as to enlist the full and open participation of those most concerned." Thus will we create "a post-capitalist economy," or else we will achieve a "stabilization" of inequality.

His other proposals for reform are co-ordinated into this plan—slum clearance and housing, regionalism and decentralization of overcrowded urban centers, beautification of the physical environment, more education, more culture in general, more recreational facilities, and so on. But his vagueness about means negates the timeliness and good intentions of these proposals.

It is obvious that "Basic Communism" requires a different form of state than that which is a "survival" of the "inorganic" past. "Basic Communism" and the power state are incompatible. However, he saw this contradiction being resolved by a process of social evolution. The power state was gradually being supplanted by the service state. In other words, the state based on force and oppressive class rule was dying out because it was inadequate to meet the requirements of the "new integration." In its place, the service state, which ministers to the needs of the whole community, was developing. Signs of this development are apparent in the expansion of the functions and services provided by the Department of Agriculture. To speak cryptically, the Department of Agriculture and departments of sanitation in the municipalities are crowding out the police and the War Department.

The role that Marxists, for instance, have given to political action in social change, Mumford attributes to an unspecified process of evolution. Instead of men and political parties and classes acting to effect change, changes have just been taking place of themselves. This "post-Marxian" view is, to Mumford, superior to Marxian eschatology. However, Mumford is himself an eschatologist. Mumford will have no traffic with the Marxian concept of the withering away of the state. But what he has actually believed in and has promulgated amounts to

nothing less than the prediction that capitalism, itself, is withering away. Herein we see why Mumford has been so quixotic
concerning the study of the means necessary to achieve his ends.
The reason he has been so cavalier about the crucial question of
political power is now laid bare.

Mumford has written grandiose and well-intentioned plans
for a better society. He tells us that these plans must be put into
effect. He advocates no concrete political action. Rather, he
proposes that the best minds get together and plot the next step
for the evolution of the progressive tendency. Such attitudes
are at the root of his reformism. This was embodied in his book,
The Culture of the Cities. Reviewers hailed this work as a major
contribution to knowledge; it can be more precisely described
as the classic of settlement house culture. Mumford and Geddes
both have been the prophets of this kind of social reform. It is
thus that, in *The Culture of the Cities*, he expresses regret
because society has neglected to provide adequate meeting halls
for the workers, as if that would have been an important contribution to the solution of those political problems that the
worker must face. Similarly, Patrick Geddes once applauded
the Boy Scout movement, both as the solution of the problem
of the wayward boy and as a means of increasing a love of nature
among boys. It is in these features of both Mumford and Geddes
that we can most clearly discern the influence of Le Play. Given
to regrets about the past, Mumford has lamented that the
influence of Le Play has not been strongly felt. The basis of that
lament was almost removed.

Press dispatches informed us that De Maistre was revived
in Petain's France as a leading ideologist. Le Play might have
been similarly resurrected. His ideas were made to order for
Marshal Petain. The Hero of Verdun tried to substitute for the
great words of the French Revolution—Liberty, Fraternity,
Equality—those of *work, family, nation*. The trinity of Le Play
was *place, work, people* (or *folk*).

Herein we see some of the involutions and implications of
Mumford's faith in the organic. To repeat, these are primarily
based on a secularization of the Catholic conception of the

unity of society in God. And they serve the role of masking the class character of society. The "organic" here is a fog, a mist, a camouflage, concealing the naked and brutal facts of societies, past and present.

v

Today, Mumford's reformism is bankrupt. He is in the same quandary as are the liberals he has condemned. How did he meet the crisis imposed by the Second World War? He returned to his origins. *Men Must Act* and *Faith for Living* read very much like *The Coming Polity*, written by Patrick Geddes and Victor Branford during the First World War. They saw that struggle as a struggle of humanity against "Prussic" materialism.[14] Matching their style and thought, Mumford substituted for "Prussic" materialism the phrase "pragmatic liberalism." Employing this phrase in very much the same way that they used "Prussic" materialism, Mumford finally voided it of all sense. He attacked as "pragmatic liberals," directly or by implication, John Dewey, the editors of *Common Sense*, General Gamelin, Neville Chamberlain, Sidney Hook, Leon Blum, the editorial board of *The New Republic*, John Steinbeck, Sir Samuel Hoare, Daladier, Pierre Laval, Charles Beard, Erskine Caldwell, John Haynes Holmes, Machiavelli, Voltaire, Rousseau, and others; not even Goethe escaped this moral infection, for did not he shelve unanswerable problems of love and knowledge in order to write "a well conceived program of public works." "The pragmatic liberal" became for Mumford a label that included just about everyone, living or dead, with whom he disagrees. Repeating the ideas of De Maistre, he saw in modern rational thinking the seeds of a cult of power or of domination. To it— "pragmatic liberalism"—he juxtaposed "ideal liberalism." He confessed his inability to define and describe "ideal liberalism,"

[14] Geddes and Branford praised De Maistre in *The Coming Polity* for having presented "a view of life and the world inimical to the Prussian cult of force." Life and history are too ironical to the views of these men; for De Maistre, inimical to the cult of Prussianism, was the master of the tradition behind the rightist groups that supported Marshal Petain, and collaborated with Hitler.

but told us that it constituted the great human tradition, which had persisted from the time of the Hebrews to the eighteenth century. It encompassed love, the ideals of abstract truth, justice and freedom, and the Roman conception of impersonal law. In order to defend his interpretation of "ideal liberalism" he had to tear the facts of history into shreds. Vague and muddled, he even reduced "ideal liberalism" to an empty ritualism. Thus, *Faith for Living* informed us that "for a few centuries mankind was free from the worst effects of Machiavellianism by the fact that the church, even where it, too, was seizing power, had created a ceremonial of hypocrisy; velvet gloves on the iron hand." This, of course, is more compatible with dignity and justice than the social theories of Jean Jacques Rousseau, the army of revolutionary France—which defended youthful democracy in the eighteenth century—the history of Charles Beard, or the philosophy of John Dewey. His case against empiricism was stated on the worst possible level, that of mere name-calling and abuse. He turned modern empirical thought into a kind of sin against the moral conscience of mankind, and fascism became the punishment visited upon it because of this sin. Here he reiterated on a vulgar plane the same kind of charges that De Maistre and De Bonald leveled against the ideologies of the Enlightenment. This is one of the ways in which Mumford returned to his origins. Today he is still close to his origins, although he has shifted some of his emphasis; this, we have seen.

Mumford offers no real ideas to refute. He has only muddled assertions and abuse left in his arsenal. He tried to write a program for society and a faith for living. This contained much of the old Mumford, and a few additions. He wanted labor camps for youth and compulsory service of the total citizenry for the service of the community. He argued for the rebirth of the family (Le Play) and proposed as part of the basis for a "faith for living," the keeping of family diaries and the advice that the housewife bake her own bread rather than buy it at the village bakery. At the same time he advocated the expansion of "life-giving" community enterprises, he also proposed an economy of sacrifice (scarcity). He told us that all sacrifices would be justified if we could save our immaterial heritage and our institutions. But he was unable to tell us precisely and with historical accuracy what our immaterial heritage was and is. And he himself implicitly sought the overthrow of institutions by his call for an economy of scarcity. Now, in his latest work, he wants to reconstruct the world by reconstructing personalities. His proposals are more vague than ever. War economy created spurious prosperity; it has nothing to do with a balanced economy. Yes, he is more vague than ever.

To say that Lewis Mumford is confused does not exhaust the discussion of what he says and proposes. He is one of the outstanding spokesmen among the war intellectuals. To those of us who have said that this war will not solve the major problems of our society and that it is a war for empire and world domination, the war intellectuals replied that the Second World War was not a continuation of its predecessor, on a new stage, but totally different in character. The irony of their assertion resides in the fact that they have been unable to find new reasons to justify this war and to rationalize the United States' participation in it. Thus they have been forced to justify a new kind of war by using the arguments and slogans of an old war. Mumford set for himself the task of finding a metaphysics for the Second World War. His metaphysics are scarcely lasting as long as the war.

Opposition to Mumford's ideas and proposals does not, as some like him insist, mean defense of fascism. Mumford himself is totally contradictory on what constitutes the nature of fascism. For instance, he does not even cite what has been historically a major purpose of all fascist dictatorships—the total destruction of all working-class organizations. He does not answer these crucial questions: What kinds of economic and social situations give rise to fascism? What is the social composition of fascist movements? What are the political mechanics whereby fascism comes to power? [15] He derides those who ask

15 I have stated my own views concerning the answer to these questions in my article, "Ignazio Silone," in The Southern Review, Spring, 1939.

these questions and tells us that fascism is a disease, a meta-physical state of mind, and a barbaric reversion. Now, fascism does afford endless material for the psychiatrist, but Mumford does not give us any help here, even though he does see fascism as a psychosis. And, above all, he does not relate fascism as a social phenomenon to fascism as a psychiatric problem. His descriptions of, and assertions about, fascism contradict one another and are wholly confusing. He who confuses us concerning this question only helps to disarm us for the real struggle that we must make against this very real menace.

Mumford today is but one more example of the intellectual whose own confusions mirror the collapse of reformism. The essentially reformist program of the Popular Front resulted in many elements of the Left losing their independence of action and their socialist programs. They soon lost their will to act. Thus shorn of both program and action, they had only one remaining alternative to save them from their own political bankruptcy—war. This, now, has not saved them either. The reformist elements of the Left had no camp to go to except that of war. Mumford reflected this situation. He wrote his *metaphysics* of the war. But he did not tell us how to implement what he said. He still does not.

Politics is serious. It is characteristic of many of our intellectuals, including Lewis Mumford, that they have never learned this truism. Any program for war or for social reform which does not carry the means of implementation is frivolous. And Mumford has never been concerned with this particular feature of social reform. We have seen where he has been led as a consequence.

The French Jacobin, Saint-Just, wrote on the eve of the Thermidor: "It is only those who are in battles who win them, and it is only those who are powerful who profit by them." Because the intellectuals of 1917 and 1918 never learned this lesson, they woke up with an intense after-war headache. In such a condition they denounced the war they had previously pronounced a holy crusade. Lewis Mumford reversed the process. He denounced the Second World War in advance, and then after the "peace" ended he woke up with a headache. He wished we would all experience his headache. He told us that unless we did, civilization was doomed. Events of the war have tested Mr. Mumford. In 1940 I said that there are many answers to Mr. Mumford. I cited one. Before the First World War, Rosa Luxembourg said: "Democracy acquires greater chances of survival as the socialist movement becomes sufficiently strong to struggle against the reactionary consequences of world politics and the bourgeois desertion of democracy. He who would strengthen democracy should want to strengthen socialism and not weaken the socialist movement. He who renounces the struggle for socialism renounces both the labor movement and democracy." The present war has confirmed this.

1940
(Revised, 1945)

Mortimer J. Adler: A Provincial Torquemada

EVERY TIME I SEE the name of Mortimer J. Adler, I am reminded of a remark Samuel Johnson made about an eighteenth-century poet: "He was dull in a new way, and that made many think him great." As a contemporary obscurantist and obfuscator, Mortimer J. Adler bows to no one—not even to Waldo Frank. He writes with a pomposity that some people mistake for profundity; his scholarship is superficial; and although he is fond of using the word logic, his reasoning is weak, even shabby. With the possible exception of Bishop Manning, Adler might be called the leading American fellow traveler of the Roman Catholic Church. The role he now plays suggests a parallel with John Strachey. In the days when John Strachey was fellow-traveling, he is reported to have been asked why he did not join the Communist Party. His answer was that he was not good enough to be a Communist. Why doesn't Adler undergo baptism? Would he give Strachey's answer to the question? He reminds me of a man who stands by a swimming pool and watches his friends enjoy themselves in the water. They see that he is anxious to join them, and shout for him to come in because the water is fine. He poises himself to dive, but, at the last moment, he recoils. He cannot force himself to make that dive into the unknown, which will get him wet. After fits and starts, encouragements and exhortations, he turns away from the pool and goes off urging other people to go swimming because the water is fine.

The success and influence of Mortimer J. Adler indicates clearly that his dullness is new to many people. Obviously, it is something new to such intellects as Robert Maynard Hutchins and Clifton P. Fadiman. But to me, it is pretty stale stuff. Whenever I pick up anything Adler has written, I am determined to read every word. But I quickly get the point he is driving at and I realize that this is where I came in. All Adler has to say is like my mother's milk to me. Long, long ago I was fed it from a better source than Mr. Adler. It was not digestible then, and it is less digestible now when Adler feeds it to me.

One of Mortimer J. Adler's fundamental postulates is the following: A proposition that cannot be demonstrated is more true than a proposition that can be. In other words, basic truths are self-evident and not subsumable to empiric proof. A philosophy of empiricism or scientific method is heresy. Positivism, reaching its worst state of degradation in the pragmatism of John Dewey, is not only heresy—it is a heresy which leads squarely into totalitarianism. Positivistic university teachers in the United States are a bigger menace than Hitler, Mussolini, and Franco. How does Adler defend this position? By begging questions. By removing his postulates from the realm where they can be demonstrated. By name-calling. And what are his self-evident truths? Those which are postulated in the dogma of the Roman Catholic Church.

Several years ago, Adler composed a metaphysics of the movies titled *Art and Prudence*. In that book he wrote: "In the deepest sense, all contemporary European societies are democratic, whether their government is republican and legislation is representative, as in England, France, and the United States, or whether it is totalitarian, and the rule is by a dictator or by a single party, as in Germany, Italy, and Russia." Further, he stated: "The importance of the ministry of propaganda in Italy and Germany indicates the democratic aspect of these societies." In a footnote in the same book, he even fell for Stalin's new constitution. Today, Mortimer J. Adler has come forward as a true defender of democracy. He is defending democracy, not only against Hitler, but, even more so, against President Conant of Harvard, John Dewey of Teachers College, and sundry others. He is even composing a metaphysics of democracy. Perhaps in his metaphysics of democracy he will write as acutely on the movies as he wrote on democracy in his metaphysics of the movies.

Adler's critique of modern thought and science does not differ in any fundamental sense from such books as Gilson's *The Unity of Philosophical Experience*, Maritain's *True Humanism*, or Father D'Arcy's *The Nature of Belief*.[1] Adler and his co-thinking Catholic philosophers all sing the same tune: Modern thought is heretical, and only they possess the true belief; the true belief is self-evident; because of the influence of heretics in the last several centuries, modern man is unhappy, modern society is in chaos, and modern thought is in a blind alley; man must believe as they believe. From Adler's premises, you can explain anything ex post facto: you can explain the reasons for any phenomenon from the defeat of France in 1940 to women wearing short skirts. However, I observe that these men who have the true belief seem utterly unable to predict. The true belief appears to give them no aid in predicting the future. All they seem able to do is to prophesy doom in generalizations that do not even glitter. Their progammatic conceptions are a hodge-podge. For society, they want a new City of God that is not the old City of God, and yet it is like the old City of God, and still, it isn't quite the old City of God. For modern philosophy they want a return to the Absolute. That means putting science in its place and restoring theology as the queen bee in the intellectual hive. A philosophical ally of this group, Berdyaev, suggests their philosophical program in the following sentence: "The existence of philosophy presupposes an appropriate philosophical mode of cognition as distinct from a scientific one."[2] And Berdyaev, following Max Scheler, considers science as more or less the revolt of the slaves. There is a class struggle of the mind between religion and science, and

[1] I am here considering Gilson's own positive views, and not his excellent scholarly researches on medieval thought.
[2] *Solitude and Society* by Nicolas Berdyaev. New York, 1938, page 16.

philosophy is in the tragic position of the centrist. None of these thinkers, Catholics and fellow travelers, have any originality of mind. They run in pat and settled grooves, and they mix up vagueness and sentimentality with appeals for authoritarianism. Their authoritarianism is defended by all the stale arguments for reaction. They use a religious glow and the historic prestige of medieval and classic philosophers as a camouflage for this authoritarianism. But an authoritarian doctrine needs more than arguments borrowed from Aquinas if it is to be implemented. It needs force. That these new medievalists are prepared for force to uphold their superior Reason is made clear in Maritain's *True Humanism*. There Maritain, in reality, defends the persecution of "heretics" by state coercion. At the present time, Mortimer J. Adler is merely a provincial Torquemada without an Inquisition.

When these men talk of the past of the Church, they idealize that past. They find sophistries to support the persecution of heretics. They prate about the unity of medieval society while forgetting that there was disunity as well as unity in that form of society. They are still playing the role of intellectual coroners and are issuing endless death certificates to those poor misguided fellows—the nominalists.

The historian Gibbon wrote: "The Church of Rome defended by violence the empire which she had acquired by fraud." Here is an aspect of history that fails to interest Adler. But he does have one characteristic in common with many of the early Christians. They wanted their cake and they wanted to eat it, too. The Emperor Constantine, for instance, waited until he was on his death bed to be baptized. Adler is still delaying his baptism.

1940

The Short Story

A PAPER READ AT THE FIRST AMERICAN WRITERS CONGRESS

I BELIEVE that revolutionary criticism has been particularly negligent in the field of the short story, and not without cause. For the short story does not lend itself readily to that species of over-politicalized and ideologically schematized criticism that has been too dishearteningly frequent in the literary sections of revolutionary journals. The short-story writer, because of the obvious limitations of space, does not possess the same liberties as does the novelist. Consequently he often discovers that the short story does not permit him to say all he has to say, and that he is limited to dealing in compressed experiences and single, or at best, a few impressions. Hence he must often rely on a technique of indirection, and he must utilize implicit, rather than explicit, methods. And to date there are several revolutionary critics who have not clearly revealed that they possess the equipment to deal with implication. Because of these reasons I think the short story can, perhaps, be considered as a test of the literary perceptibilities of our critics.

Putting aside esthetic considerations for the moment and considering the development of literary traditions, we can note the tendency to develop in terms of a succession of patterns, elements of one pattern tending to be assimilated into the succeeding pattern, while other elements are rejected, and so on, in a continuous process.

For purposes of illustration, I might refer, in passing, to the Negro in American writing. One pattern of the Negro in American writing is the Uncle Remus story of the dark-

skinned Southern Handy Andy. This pattern presents a vaude-
vilized conception of the Negro, portrays him as obsequious,
shiftless, childishly humorous and simple, and makes him a
subject of comedy which, as we know, slurs and distorts the
story of the tragic history of the Negro in capitalist America.
This pattern established a norm of types, habits, characteristics,
language, a residuum of conceptions, attitudes, and the like,
which was assumed to be the "spirit" of the Negro. Even to
this date the Uncle Remus pattern of the Negro has not worn
thin in American popular writing and in many American conceptions of the Negro. We meet this pattern, dressed up in
spats, in *The Saturday Evening Post* stories of Octavius Roy
Cohen. We are tortured by this conception in the movies and
in the radio skit of Amos and Andy. And we find that in Stark
Young's *So Red the Rose* the slaves are treated in terms of this
pattern or else they are considered as "bad niggers."

While it is easy for us to dismiss writing of this type from
a strictly literary point of view, we are inept if we do likewise
from a sociological viewpoint. For it quite clearly reflects a class
attitude. The Uncle Remus pattern is a combination of the
conventions forced upon the Negro to permit, on one hand,
some harmonious interaction between the Negro and the privileged class of whites living on his back, and, on the other, a
wish fulfillment of what that privileged class desires the Negro
to be. In the relationships between a privileged class and an
oppressed class a set of conventions always develops and guides
the relationships between the two classes. In time, members of
the privileged class will tend to identify these conventions,
and the necessary habits they create, with the supposed essential nature of the oppressed class. They will then view the
conduct that is canalized by these conventions as stemming
not from objective social relationships but from a myth called
the basic human nature of the oppressed. This is what has been
done in the writing that treats the Negro in terms of the Uncle
Remus pattern. We can note that this pattern contains similarities with other writing where there is a condition of master and
slave, oppressor and oppressed. Thus there is a similarity be-

tween the Uncle Remus stories of the Negro and the stage Irishmen in such nineteenth-century Irish novels as those by Charles Lever and by Samuel Lover. Similarities even extend further. Thus, the writing about children by adults is also of the same nature. Booth Tarkington's *Penrod,* for instance, is put into the same kind of mold, and it is a combination of certain conventions necessary for the intercourse between children and certain types of parents, on one hand, and, on the other hand, of a wish fulfillment or an adult fantasy about childhood.

To continue, another pattern of the Negro in American writing might be termed that of the American primitive, presented in such characterizations as those found in the writings of Julia Peterkin and DuBose Heyward, and in Marc Connelly's play, *Green Pastures.* A third pattern is the Harlem Negro, found in novels like Carl Van Vechten's *Nigger Heaven;* in Rudolph Fisher's rather inept treatment of Harlem's middle class and its intellectuals, *The Walls of Jericho;* and in Claude McKay's story of a Pullman porter, *Home to Harlem.* A fourth pattern, now in the offing, is that of the Negro proletariat; a forerunner of this literary development is Langston Hughes.[1]

These patterns of the Negro in American writing follow a shifting in class relationships and social conditions in which the Negro is a factor, and they reveal these changes and shiftings. And if we view American writing as a whole, it will be obvious, I think, that there has been a diversity of such patterns. Furthermore, we will find that there is an irregularity in their development, influence, efficacy or lack of efficacy, and we will note that they intersect and become a kind of kaleidoscope. In addition, these patterns condition the manner in which we apprehend and perceive characters and events in the American scene. For instance, inane and inept patterns still persist and are often more influential determining factors in the crystallization and reinforcement of popular attitudes than we should like them to be.

Besides the external or social factors conditioning and quali-

[1] Since this paper was written, Richard Wright has appeared on the literary scene. His work fits into this account and shows a further stage of this change.

fying the development of literature, there are also the internal, or literary, ones. And just as we are able to note the unevenness and irregularity in the development and life of social patterns, so are we able to perceive a corresponding unevenness of literary influences. One obvious example that can be cited is the persisting influence of the romantic tradition in English poetry, and the manner in which it has become a part of our language and our stylistic habits.

One of the influencing factors in American writing that requires some mention here is the plot short story, which was, until fairly recently, a dominant American literary form. The plot short story was built upon a mechanical formula, and as such it was extremely constricting. It demanded that life, as represented in the short story, be so ordered and arranged that it meet the requirements of the form rather than that the form be adapted to reveal the aspects of life a writer chose to utilize. The central demand in this form was that of conflict, based upon rising action and a clash of opposing views, which created a mounting suspense and was resolved in the denouement. The highest type of conflict for the plot short story was often conceived to be moral conflict. Frequently in plot short stories the characters were not convincing as human beings, but rather they impressed one as appendages to moral codes and points of view, and these codes and points of view were rooted in the ideology which is the intellectual bodyguard of capitalist democracy.

It is perhaps more than a mere fortuity that the revolt from the plot short story developed and attained some popularity at a time when there was an increasingly apparent contradiction between the hopes of the American dream and the manner in which human destinies unraveled in actual life. In other words, the contradictions between ideals and activity began to be apparent in American life, and people began to perceive that they were being betrayed by the American dream. The first works in that literature of realism and social protest which has come to be the dominant literary tradition in twentieth-century American writing, began a literary process of upsetting and overturning familiar patterns in American social thought and in literature. The happy ending became the unhappy ending. The plot short story became the plotless short story. Sin, instead of virtue, was rewarded, as in *Sister Carrie*. Success led to discontent rather than content, as in *Windy MacPherson's Son*. In the stories of Ring Lardner, the popular heroes of the sports page were cut into with bitter, unrelenting, and cruelly true irony, and sarcasm.

This literary revolt opened the floodgates for an inundation of new literary material that permitted, and still does permit, us to see many aspects of American life and American experience as if with new eyesight. What this writing has done, basically, is to assess the cost of American capitalist democracy in terms of human destinies and human suffering and frustrations. It has given expression to social pressures—the social pressures of new racial and class groupings seeking self-expression, self-understanding—that seeks to publicize a sense of its life, its sufferings, its problems, its aspirations, desires. Although we can see this development more clearly in the novel than in the short story, it is apparent in both forms. In the short story, we catch glimpses, states of mind, pictures of scenes, environments, atmospheres, the language of this life that hitherto had been unexpressed or unsatisfactorily expressed in American writing. In these last years then, the short story has been introducing us to a new kind of American life, to the life of poor farmers and sharecroppers in backward rural areas, to the scenes, sights, and dialects of the urban streets, to the feelings of Slavic immigrants, the problems and discontents of sweat-shop workers, the resentments and oppressions of the factory proletariat, the conduct and aspirations of revolutionary organizers, the attitudes of Negro intellectuals toward white folks, the traditions and backgrounds of labor, the brutality of the prize ring and the life behind it. In brief, it has been dipping us down toward the bottom of the so-called American melting pot. And, needless to state, both implicitly and explicitly, there is noticeable in some of this writing a revolutionary direction.

The basic inadequacy in many of the new revolutionary short

stories is, I believe, a lack of what might be called internal conviction. Thus, the authors seek to express a revolutionary point of view or a feeling and, instead of making their aim functional within the story so that the aim impresses the reader as a natural and integral aspect of the story, it seems to be glued on. In the most obvious stories it has been glued to the ending as a slogan or revolutionary direction sign that possesses no coherent and vital or necessary relation to the body of the story. Another related deficiency in revolutionary stories is that they have been too generalized. Thus, there has been any number of generalized short stories dealing with hunger, suffering, oppression, unenlivened by the kind of details, observations, and flashes of insight that would give these stories concreteness and inculcate into them a sense of these undeniable concomitants of a capitalistic civilization. As a result, these stories ring a bell, but its echo dies quickly—and the stories are quickly forgotten. They are exhausted as soon as they have been read. There has been any number of other stories seeking to express not revolutionary attitudes and sentiments, but rather to reflect aspects of American life. And in these, too, there are often noticeable deficiencies. Thus, the influence of Sherwood Anderson on the short story has become so strong as to have caused what might be termed a Sherwood Anderson school. This school of writing might be termed the I-Am-Dumb school. Again, the mannerisms and methods of Ernest Hemingway have been imitated in a rather feeble manner, and the quality that gives to some of his stories their genuine merit—that is, Hemingway's sensibility—is lacking. The result is that the imitators' stories are mere shells without feeling, without content, without any justification for their having been written. Ring Lardner has likewise had his imitators, and their results have been equally depressing. However, I think it will be more rewarding for us to consider not merely stories that can be criticized so easily, but rather to discuss a diverse group of short stories of some merit.

The first story I shall consider here is "My Dead Brother Comes to America" by Alexander Godin, originally printed in

the *Windsor Quarterly*. This story attempts to present the
feelings of an immigrant boy coming to America from the
famine-torn Ukraine with his mother and sisters. The author
writes, "We had lived through a heroic period of history [the
era of the Russian Civil War] without having anything of the
heroic in our natures, and many things had happened to us
during that time. Our lives had been broken into many shards."
Coming into the new world, confused, remembering the suffering and agony and starvation they had left, we see this immigrant boy fearing that this family will never again piece
together their shattered lives. And one of them has been left
behind, dead. But the mother had not told the father of this
in her letters to America. So, when the father meets them, he
has brought caps for all of the children, and there is one extra
cap. All the way home, and when they are settled in their new
home—a cramped New York apartment—the dead brother
hangs over this family like a pall and a symbol. "He, too, had
come to America." The emphasis in this story is on feeling and
atmosphere, a feeling of poignancy and tragedy, an atmosphere of bewilderment and confusion. It is a compact, moving
story written in the tradition of the Russian short story. And
we can note in it a difference between the author's use of details
and the use of details in many American short stories. In the
latter, details are piled on to attain effects and establish backgrounds and atmospheres by massed details, and by using details
suggesting the novelty of a scene and the language of the milieu
that they treat and they like. Godin uses details much more
sparingly and seeks to gain a maximum of effect from each.
Thus, the mere detail of the extra cap tells his entire story,
and the caps become a symbol. Also, this is one type of story
that extends outward in the reader's consciousness after it has
been read. It is like a door opening up to us a sense of the feeling
of the immigrant and of the background of agony and suffering
from which he has come. It emphasizes feeling, emotion and
atmosphere rather than ideology, and is the kind of story that
revolutionary critics should encourage. It reveals to us a sense
of the backgrounds of the immigrant workers and their fami-

lies, and as such, I think that it is one of the most moving contemporary stories that I have ever read.

In such a story as Nelson Algren's "So Help Me," originally printed in *Story*, we are introduced into an entirely different world, that of the hobo jungle. In brief, this is the story of the education of a young Jewish boy in the life of the hobo. He had entered this world as a kind of victim of circumstances. A school boy in Cincinnati, he had fallen in love with a girl he wanted to marry and had caused her to become pregnant. Racial and religious differences in the two families had created friction, and under the threats of the girl's father, he had hitch-hiked to Boulder Dam, hoping to find work and to send for the girl. There he had found five thousand men ahead of him waiting for five jobs, so he had gone to New Orleans, despairingly hoping to ship out. There he met a hobo with whom he went on a freight to Texas in search of work. A companion joined them, and the two hoboes played the boy for a chump, involved him in a robbery, murdered him. The story is told in monologue, and in a manner that suggests the influence of Ring Lardner. The author develops not only this particular tale but its background. As the hobo telling the story comes alive before our eyes, we perceive his lack of sentiment and disregard for love, his almost complete divorcement from the middle-class conceptions of success, and his lack of substitutions of any other conceptions for them. His only concern is to function at a human minimum from day to day, and if he can use anyone else to help him, so much the better, and the hell with what it does to them. Society did not care how it treated him. He is heedless of how he treats others. He lives, literally, in a jungle, which the author describes unrelentingly, so that it strikes us like a powerful blow in the face, and the author's irony is shaped into an effective literary instrument. As a story, "So Help Me" should classify as one assessing the cost of capitalist society, bringing before our eyes some of the lineaments, as it were, of contemporary American life, and re-creating a sense of the meaning of life, the feel, the atmosphere, of it among the lower strata of our "dollar casualties."

Originally printed in the *Anvil*, I think, Louis Mamet's "The Pension" is a story which has received well-deserved attention and praise. It stands forth like a clear light against many of those dreary, unfelt, and unrealized, if sincere, short stories of the proletariat which have studded little magazines. Basically, it strives to represent the relationship of the machine worker to his machines and to his employers in a capitalist system. The characters are referred to by the numbers of their machines, an effective literary device for establishing an overtone of the factory atmosphere. The protagonist, Pop, or Number Five, is an old and competent worker who has only six months more to work before he will receive his pension. Suddenly he is assigned to machine Number Twenty-nine, a machine that has invariably crippled workers. He pleads against this assignment, and his foreman seeks to intervene, but orders are orders, and the reader is led to understand that they have been issued with the knowledge that they will cause the old man to lose his pension. The meaning of this loss is crippled old age and poverty, with the addition of nostalgic sorrows. These orders impress on Pop's brain a lesson in capitalistic economy, and he realizes that he is to be washed aside as so much dripping and wasted oil from a machine. He commits suicide in order to avoid this final degradation and to provide insurance money for his aging wife. His executive at the factory expresses regret, but orders are orders, production costs must be kept down, schedules fulfilled, and at least the old man is now a problem for the city morgue instead of for the factory executive. A new man is to be put on machine Twenty-nine, and he will probably be crippled as his predecessors have been. The story is told in an impressionistic manner, and while this method has often been used ineffectively in America, in this case it is handled with nothing short of brilliance. Under headings chronicling the time of day, the incidents are etched in revealing dialogue and with a few hasty but telling strokes of descriptions, so that there is scarcely a wasted word in the story. And the social implications are revealed through human terms and come to us as inevitable potentialities of the situation rather than the obverse.

In his story, "Kneel to the Rising Sun," Erskine Caldwell proceeds on a fresh track. In the most effective of his earlier stories, he had succeeded in presenting to us the feeling, the gusto, the burlesque, and the grim tragedy in the lives of the milieu he writes about. In this story he states a social problem in the terms and lives of similar characters. Briefly, the problem is that of the sharecroppers in their relationship with their exploiters and the social system of which both they and their exploiters are a part. The principal characters are Clem, a Negro sharecropper with will, courage, and an independent spirit; Lonnie, a white sharecropper who has been reduced by poverty to a state of abjectness and who is made craven by subservience to the sentiments expressed in the ideology of his exploiters. Their common landlord is Arch, another Erskine Caldwell character, whose quirk of character, or hobby, is that of cutting off the tails of dogs and saving them in a large trunk. Arch has been waiting for years for an opportunity to "get" Clem, who is a "bad nigger." Arch keeps his sharecroppers on a starvation diet. Driven by hunger, Lonnie's blind father wanders off at night in search of food, falls into the hog trough, and is killed by the hogs. Clem assists Lonnie in searching for the father, and after his body is found, Lonnie, at Clem's insistence, awakens Arch. There is a resultant argument between Arch and Clem, with Lonnie as a quaking spectator. Clem defends himself from attack, and this defense gives Arch his opportunity. He rushes off to summon a lynch mob. Clem explains to Lonnie that he can escape if Lonnie will aid him. Lonnie cannot make up his mind. When the lynch mob arrives, Lonnie betrays his potential comrade, and the lynch mob sadistically pumps the Negro full of lead. The outlines of the story are clear. Had Lonnie helped Clem, the latter would not have been murdered. The implication is equally lucid: it is the unity of black and white sharecroppers in self-defense against the system exploiting them both. And as in Louis Mamet's story, the incidents are unfolded with no sacrifice of the human terms and personalities involved, so that the conviction in the stories is internal, and hence effective, rather than external. The only criticism I should offer is one that I think can be made of various other Caldwell writings. The element of horror is overdrawn. Thus, the death of the blind father is extremely grisly, and it tends to lessen the second and more important horror in the story, Clem's murder. It is my opinion, at least, that the author might have saved the first grisly death for a second story, contrived the argument between Clem and Arch by other means, and saved his impact for the lynching of Clem. But even with this criticism, I think that "Kneel to the Rising Sun" is one of Erskine Caldwell's most effective and satisfying stories.

Although Ben Field's "Cow" was printed in *Hound and Horn* almost four years ago, it is still remembered. The hero in this story is a physically powerful, mentally alert unemployed Jewish carpenter with the Spartan temperament of a true revolutionary. Possessed of a contagious zest for living, his effect upon those with whom he works as a farm hand is best indicated by a quotation: ". . . our fellow worker of the summer, who had come in our midst like a bomb and, bursting himself, planted his fragments in some of us, perhaps, forever." The creation of a sense of such a character, with his energy and aliveness, is always a difficult task, and I think that Ben Field succeeded so well that when the hero dies of an accident it is a moving tragedy. Also, the story is extremely rich in overtones and in apt metaphors, which seem to fit and flow along with the narrative. As we read, we catch overtone after overtone, a simile describing the moon as "like a broken thumbnail," conversations of the characters that compress their estimation of their own lives and their rough and ready philosophies into a few quick lines. And to my knowledge, this is one of the few short stories treating revolutionary characters that does not fit into Michael Gold's apt description—"stooge fiction."

Whittaker Chambers' "Can You Hear Their Voices?," printed in the old monthly, *New Masses*, has come to occupy a place in revolutionary writing similar to that held by Paul Peter's *Stevedore* in the revolutionary drama. Chambers' characters are farmers suffering from the depression and the drought, looking hopelessly upon their parched and unyielding land, seeing their cattle die of thirst, watching their babies hover near death, because of lack of milk, noticing the pinch of hunger in the cheeks of their wives. The author aims to bring out clearly the basic social alignments and causes of this predicament, and to describe the effective and unified direct action taken by these farmers to prevent themselves and their families from dying like the dogs of a broken-down economic system. With an ending similar to that of *Stevedore,* the story makes for exciting and stirring reading. But in his effort to present essential and basic economic factors, it seems to me that Whittaker Chambers slipped into obviousness in certain points of his story. Thus, there is a brief scene describing the way in which the local authorities frantically telephoned a senator in Washington for aid to clog and halt the rising action and rebellion of the farmers, and here the ring is too familiar. Also, in order to bring in a number of elements of topical interest, the author could not in his space bring out sufficiently all the potentialities of his material. Thus, during the midst of the action there is reference to the failure of the local bank; this hangs in the air, a thread not drawn tightly into the story. But despite these criticisms, the story is alive as a piece of fiction and re-creates a sense of the impact of the social system, and of the meaning of the drought and the depression in the rural areas.

Langston Hughes' "Home from the Ways of White Folks" is another story of lynching. It tells of a sensitive and talented young Negro musician who returns to his home in a small Missouri town, suffering from consumption. In Europe he had been treated as a human being. In his home town, he is just another "uppity nigger" to the white loafers. He becomes acquainted with a white school teacher, with music the sole basis of their acquaintanceship. One night when they meet on the main street and pause to talk of music, the white loafers attack him. The woman screams. Her scream has only one meaning—rape. And when we read of this sensitive young man being beaten, stripped—his mouth choked with blood—killed, we

get a sense of the meaning of lynching. The story, written with
that warmth and richness of sensibility so characteristic of
Langston Hughes' best writing, is a clear-cut definition of the
violences potential in American life, the doors slammed in the
faces of the talented members of the author's race.

John Strachey, in *The Coming Struggle for Power*, writes,
"Literature . . . is a great sea into which for centuries have
been poured all those thoughts, dreams, fantasies, concepts,
ascertained facts which did not fit into any of the other categories of human thought. Into literature have gone philosophical
ideas too tenuous for the philosophers, dreams too literal for
plastic expression, facts too uncorrelated for science, and emotions too intertwined with the particular instance to find expression in the glorious and precise abstractions of music." In
other words, literature might be described as a reservoir of human emotions and feelings. And critically our task, not only in
the short story, but in all literary forms, is to assimilate this
material and to use it as the basis for the tradition in revolutionary American writing that we all seek to further and
develop.

1935

Thirty and Under

THE CHRONOLOGICALLY-MINDED have now dedicated to us of the younger generation a new era in which we might make our bids as contributors to the spiritual history of our times. And with the advent of the new decade there has been a fairly wholesale house cleaning of Rousseauism, romanticism, and revolutionism of all sorts and varieties. The Humanists and others have attempted to define their attitudes and to list the prerequisites of enlistment under their banner. Accepting them and their basic assumptions, we can stand shouting the words which Roosevelt used at the 1912 convention. "We stand at Armageddon and we battle for the Lord." However, a few of us wonder whether it is the Lord for whom we desire to fight. We wonder, particularly, whether or not we want to join those of our own generation who are revolting against revolt. At the present time it seems essential that some of us—those still under thirty—offer some dissent before we are completely silenced by the noise that Humanism makes.

The gathering spirit of this fresh decade is one of affirmation. The whine of the jazzed and heartbroken despair of yesterday is dying out. Futility is being effaced from the tablet of values. Moody skepticism is being castigated by devastating analysis. Younger people—among them most of the contributors to the *Saturday Review of Literature*'s recent "Thirty or Under" contest, for instance—have decided that life must have purpose, dignity, direction. We are going back to standards.

A reversion to standards in a period of confusion tempts

many into bypaths of misdirection. The sense of a positive need for a philosophy·does as much harm as it does good. The Humanist revival is sufficient proof of this fact. Inasmuch as many must have values, they have accepted ready-made ones. Dr. Babbitt's juxtaposition of generalized categories gives one a measuring rod with which we can judge and arrange. Looming in the rear of Dr. Babbitt is Mother Church, even more positive than he is. Both have their devils and their saints; both possess a complete and effective technique of castigation.

The developing positivism of faith has, as yet, not traveled past a series of generalizations, and consequently we are left as confused as ever in the face of many pressing contemporary problems. All some do is to cover a smug retreat from the contemporary situation. Mr. Harlan Hatcher, winner of *The Saturday Review* contest, discovers that we must recapture the lyric note, that we must reaffiirm humanity, and that we must grow from the traditions of the masters. He deprecates experimentalism, for instance, and states that no great literature ever grew from the clinic, without stopping to analyze modern conditions that tend to make experimentalism and freakishness a soulful necessity of escape, and, worse, tend to keep the clinics thriving. In another place he writes, "We inherit a country already quite safe for literature and art and steadily increasing in virtue. We may, therefore, spare the lash and encourage our brethren in the faith." In another, he writes, "We want to find beauty and [to] respond to it with passionate recognition." Had he stopped to consider the problems of the modern city, he might have written differently. He might have observed that we city-dwellers have been educated without the lyric emotions he wants. Dust and prairies, gravel playgrounds and artificially pretty parks, were our childhood backgrounds. Thus, when we seek to recapture the lyric note, we become frail and gently evanescent, like, say, George Dillon.

I mention this because it strikes at the heart of one of our problems. Recapturing the supposed lyric note is reversion. Our predicament requires the resolution of all techniques—art, religion, science—to the central problem of accommodating ourselves psychologically to a milieu different from all others in human history. When our younger generation grows positive, its positivism must take the form of outlining a program that will give intelligent direction to the momentum of our time. It requires not generalizations on what our belles-lettres must accomplish, but specific attitudes on a number of questions that torment and fret the mind of modern man. For one, it demands an attitude toward the capitalistic, commercial structure of modern life. Many younger people seem to believe that Mencken and Lewis solved the problem of Main Street, that they made our country safe for art. This is pure nonsense. The central fact of modern life is that we have one dominant value—money.

The Humanists reply to this fact with an insistence on an inner check. An inner check is worthless in the face of an outer situation that stresses the things which an inner discipline seeks to prevent. For instance, the Roman Catholic Church is Humanism's ally in the insistence on inner discipline. Yet for centuries now, and particularly today in America, the Church has become but a formalization. As Dr. Babbitt has illustrated, the Church in America has become part and parcel of our civilization; it has become power-hungry, with a tendency to substitute external size for an inner spirit.

When acquisitiveness is the order of the day, when the rewards go to him who diverts social resources for private exploitation, and when this condition prevails in a life that is fast and nerve-racking to the point of demanding similarly fast and nerve-racking diversion, we need more than ethical principles. The external world has been altered. Our social accommodation must be matched to this situation. In brief, the problem is as much sociological as ethical. The program of action must be detailed and constructive on specific points. Dr. Babbitt, in a recent article in *The Forum*, presented his program as follows:

1. A coming together on the basis of a Socratic definition of Humanism;
2. A conventionalizing of this definition;
3. Education in terms of this convention.

The younger generation had better stop, look, listen, and think, before selling its soul to such a program.

So far, I have gone beyond the realm of pure literary problems. As a literary generation, what are we to do? Undoubtedly, our esthetic theory must be remodeled. We are done with art for expression, with a Bohemian isolation of creative effort on a celestial island of pure subjective moodiness. Yet we are fools if we deny this for the sake of accepting an ethical art which retreats from today by way of receded yesterdays, and which saps the vigor of personal response in an arid intellectualism. We must establish better foundations. Our esthetic theory must consider art as an effort at perceiving, understanding, arranging, evaluating, and at communicating personal experiences, primarily with the purpose of comprehension. When social accommodation has become more harmonious, art will gather social purpose. It cannot be part of a synthesis until that synthesis is formed. In the meantime art plumbs and explores confusion, chaos, and disorder, to gather a surer comprehension. Art must tackle experience, not to prove ethical orders and golden proportions, but to derive all the possible meanings that can be deduced.

Where we must differ from the Humanists and from those closely akin to them is in our abnegation of finalities. While they, for instance, speak of central human experiences and qualities, anthropologists collect more files of evidence disproving all that is central and normal, reducing the Humanists and their dicta to an irritating arrogance. Modern technology and modern science have built our world. They have reordered experience. Denying this fact is futile. Denying the relativism that has resulted is contributing to a "monstrous logomachy" (the phrase is used by Dr. Babbitt). The one decisive verdict of history is the changing quality of experience, with its ability to furnish its own tools of adjustment. And the conclusion to be drawn from this is that we must, with intelligent control, attempt to work out the forces of social direction as well as we can.

In brief, the human project is an experiment that has as many meanings and purposes as there are individuals and groups. In such a situation, centrality is shifting. The good life depends on the social arrangement and on the type of expression it affords. In a commercial civilization, where the dollar is stressed and where universal acquisitiveness breeds universal suspicion, there is little question as to which problems are most important. Instead of a "civil war in the cave" of the human soul, there must be a form of social organization that directs what is most generous and social in man and that sublimates what is not. In brief, the problem of those of us who own the Thirties is more one of social attack than of ethical reversion and traditionalism.

1930

In Search of the Image

VARIOUS CRITICISMS of the imagery and stylistic habits in Edward Dahlberg's recent *Those Who Perish* call to mind certain remarks which should be of technical interest, at least, to writers and critics.

The study of an author's style, his selection of imagery, and the symbols he uses to establish his atmospheres and enrich his meanings is one which, to my knowledge, has received little contemporary popular attention. A Marxian, with sufficient time and resources, could bring forth considerable data of value and illumination from such a study. In style and the use of imagery there are a succession of traditions and conventions, following each other like waves, and these traditions and conventions follow the same course as do most methodologies. They have a beginning, when they are a novelty, and often find extensive application for their own sake and out of a sense of novelty. There follows a long or short period of crystallization, when they have their full efflorescence and when their potentialities are developed to the fullest possibility of realization. Following this, there is an approach to a point of diminishing returns. Then the values and uses that permitted the extraction of values in the period of efflorescence become matters of mere usage and habits. Conventionalization has reached a period of mechanical habit. Soon the use of this convention is like trying to suck juice from a totally dry lemon. In addition, by indirection and refraction, conventions and traditions in style and imagery are tied up with the period out of which they develop and reach their efflorescence. Implicitly, the use of imagery reflects esthetic evaluations of a period, attitudes, and, to a considerable extent, an ideology. Marx suggested this fact in a note at the end of *A Critique of Political Economy*. Speaking of Greek art, he asked the question, does it (Greek art) not exert an eternal charm? Readily granting this eternal charm of Greek art, he added that it drew upon the ideology of a period that was forever past, and that in this age of industrialization, developed by the application of scientific principles, there could be no symbolism based upon a mythology that conceived natural forces as the influence of extramundane gods living beyond the world of nature.

This type of approach, I repeat, applied to the imagery and symbolism of contemporary writing, could, I believe, be very illuminating. It is to be noted that even today the symbolism and imagery in much contemporary writing finds its source in nineteenth-century romanticism. Implicit in the use of much romantic imagery and symbolism is the assumption of dualism. Dualism assumes the bifurcation of the world into spirit and matter, and often runs into extremes of mysticism. A device developed to a high stage of perfection in romantic writing, and implicitly assuming a dualistic outlook, is that of anthropomorphism. Anthropomorphism ascribes human powers, feelings, and emotions to things not human. An implicit dualism is likewise to be found in a great portion of romantic love poetry, wherein love is conceived in spiritual terms and soul unions and the like. One of the revelations of romantic poetry was that of the wild charm and attraction of nature. The romantic movement turned men's eyes to nature and they began to see it afresh and to extract from it new emotional and esthetic values. Nature, tied up with anthropomorphism, quickly became an abundant source of imagery. One persistence of the romantic strain in contemporary writing is that dependence on nature as a source of imagery and the use of romantic labels for symbolism. For a number of us, this usage of romantic convention has reached a period of diminishing returns. To repeat, it is like sucking on a dry lemon.

I have selected illustrations of the persistence of the romantic literary conventions in contemporary writing at random. A prominent editor, reviewing a novel several months back in *Books,* described it as moving with the rhythm of the wind in the wheat fields. A few years ago the poet McKnight Black attempted in his poetry to give expression to the emotions he felt when perceiving machinery. Reading his poems it was quite apparent that one could have substituted for railroad trains and machinery the girl, the tree, the wind, and the moonlight at night, and the poems would have gained in efficacy. Very recently, Ilya Ehrenbourg offered the same criticism of many Soviet poets, complaining that in much of their poetry a knight at arms could be substituted for the Five-Year Plan without any loss of effect. Thomas Wolfe opens one of his stories with the phrase, "In the green heart of June," and for thousands of words he persists in sucking this kind of dry lemon. In his *Look Homeward Angel,* he revealed the same rather stale dependence on romantic labels, striving to gain emotional overtones with the repetition of such phrases as "the wind-grieved ghost." In another recent poem a contemporary poet used the figure of the eyelids of a suffering cave. In Hervey Allen's miserable and disgracefully overrated *Anthony Adverse* every romantic label, mannerism, and trick is used beyond the point of utter boredom. He reaches a point of total bathos and inanity when one of his characters looks piously at nature in the mood of "O." Examples of this type could be cited endlessly. These are, I feel, sufficient to suggest my point.

In dealing with style in this manner it is necessary to caution the reader that this analysis can be overrationalized and that one must not overlook the fact that there are necessary limitations of language, some necessary usages of anthropomorphism, and that language is used for evocative as well as for intellectual reasons. And also that an author does not pick his images out of a grab bag, but rather they grow out of his own background and changing experiences. But even with these admonitions it is apparent that romantic literary conventions have already passed their efflorescence and that they reflect an ideology of dualism completely dead and antiquated for many of us.

Contemporary American writers, in many cases, I believe, have either wittingly or unwittingly perceived this fact about the use of romantic symbolisms. Many of them are the products of urban life. In their immediate sensory experience they have been most affected by the sights, sounds, odors, and objects of an industrial city. In their first stages of reading particularly, they have absorbed much of the romantic poets, and in their early writing there has been some imitation of the romantics. Generally speaking, the charms and attractions of nature have been peripheral if not non-existent in their lives. Hence they often have sensed a dichotomy between the objects and sensations they have sought to describe and the language and symbolism they have inherited.

In Dahlberg's instance I believe he has either consciously or unconsciously perceived this dichotomy and that he has attempted to heal it with an original use of imagery. This imagery in many cases is derived from words and associations taken from urban sights and sounds, and from comparisons between objects that are regularly seen by those whose experience is also urban. Thus his regular use of phrases like "nedick organe," his description of a hotel awning as being "pseudo beachish." The attempt here is that of relying on a new set-up of associations and on the fashioning of a language and an imagery closely connected with his subject matter. Therefore criticism of his imagery is meaningless if made ex-cathedra and without reference to his intentions. To my knowledge, the only critic or reviewer who has clearly perceived this intention behind his imagery has been Robert Cantwell.

Various reviewers have commented upon the influence of Proust in Dahlberg's writing, and this opens up a second question of associated interest here. Proust always struggled to achieve precise effects. If he sought to describe a railroad journey he had taken, he did not seek to describe any railroad journey, or the obvious sights and sounds he had experienced or might have experienced on any railroad journey. On the contrary, he sought to give his readers a sense of the specific and particular railroad journey, and none other. With Proust the meaning of recapturing a sense of things past was not that of evoking generalized memories of obvious categories but rather of bringing to the printed page a sense of the specific objects, of specific associations, sensations and feelings that were evoked in definite atmospheres, and not in other atmospheres similar but not precisely the same. Dahlberg seeks to achieve the same type of effect. Critics have commented upon a sense of strain in his writing. This sense of strain is the concomitant of his type of sensibility. He strains and struggles to achieve precise and specific effects. When he sets a character walking down a street, he does not try to evoke the familiar sights and sounds of any street and the generalized sort of responses these would evoke in any character of a certain background and a certain grouping or class. Rather, he tries to give his readers a sense of that specific street, and of a specific character whose reactions are not wholly like those of any other characters. Such effects are achieved by the selection of unique and highly distinguishable details. And his use of imagery is also put into the service of this intention. The major effect of Proust on his work is that of stimulating this type of literary intention, and it is a wholly legitimate and non-imitative one.

There is a third question of literary technique of equal relevance here. A number of contemporary or near-contemporary writers, who have had a widespread technical influence, have attempted to perfect a literary device that can be described as telescoping. In other words, they have attempted in their writing to compress description of objects, the sensations called forth by these objects in their characters, and the selection of these objects in the manner in which the eye sees them, jumping from one to another. Among such writers are Joyce and Eliot. Their skill with this device is best illustrated by a comparison of their descriptions with those of, say, a writer like Dickens, who set down his description in a more formal pattern and more in consonance with what has since become composition-course dicta of unity, coherence, and emphasis. Dahlberg also puts his use of imagery into the service of telescoping objects and sensations together.

Criticism of his imagery must then be made in terms of whether he gives one a sense of the things he sets out to establish. In his use of imagery and symbols there is revealed a brilliant originality. And he has been able by these means—much more successfully than many of us who are his contemporaries —to endow his books with a sense of atmospheres and background. When he has been successful with these devices, as he is in the final chapter of *Those Who Perish,* the writing is considerably enriched. And the criticism of his use of imagery should be made in these terms. To achieve in any number the kinds of effects he seeks to gain, a long book is required, so that the progress of the narrative is not too impeded with the building of atmospheres and the establishment of a sense of concrete and unique details. And *Those Who Perish* was too short a book to bear this kind of burden. Secondly, all the images and associations are not of equal relevance, and some of them, though brilliant in themselves, fail to achieve a sense of the things he seeks to describe. In other words, there is a certain amount of inequality in the relevance of all his metaphors. And those that are irrelevant are subject to criticism. This, however, is a different matter from criticizing him because he uses imagery. The intention is wholly valuable if used with a proper sense of proportion.

To some, such a lengthy discussion of these matters may seem to be mere formalism. The ideal of a writer is that of presenting his fiction in such a manner that the reader will feel that this is not merely a book he is reading, but that, on the contrary, it is an actual unfolding of life. Bad writing, inappropriate style, and such factors tend to destroy this illusion in a book, and if these occur repeatedly the reader is often inclined to put aside the book. Because of this, stylistic and technical discussion in criticism, if approached as an aspect of criticism and not as an end in itself, is not vain formalism. And it is one of the merits of

Dahlberg's writing that he is conscious of the problems of style and technique and is trying to solve them.

In addition, each writer must convince and educate his readers in terms of his own sensibilities and attitudes. It is characteristic of good writing that it eschews a dependence upon the literary conventions and labels and symbolisms of other writers, but, on the contrary, seeks to present fresh imagery and additional understanding of character, and a fresh sense of life. If readers ask to be given only what they already know, and are anxious merely to have repeated for them symbolisms that have already been developed and conventionalized, they are reading at a low level and derive little new understanding from writers. Therefore, matters of style, of technique, of symbolism, are constant problems facing the writer. A greater familiarity with them on the part of readers, and a more thoroughgoing interest and understanding of these problems by critics and reviewers, add to the total literary atmosphere and tend to create conditions conducive to better writing.

1934

Letter to a Young Writer

Dear Mr. ——

You ask me for advice. Advice is the one thing that I am the least inclined to try to give anyone. It is seldom of any real assistance. People generally have to find things out for themselves; and this is eminently so in the case of young writers. Therefore I fear that all I can say to you will consist merely of a few truisms.

In writing, anyone who is sincere and serious should forget about giving precedence to the ideas of the market and the element of commerce in literature, and he should try to write about the material he knows best in the most truthful and honest manner he can. I think a young writer should read as much as possible and as widely as he can. One can learn more about the problems of writing from reading about the lives of writers than from the formal treatises on the subject. One should read good biographies of writers and also their letters. I should recommend particularly the letters of Chekhov and of Dostoievsky. If you will read the lives and the letters of writers, you will find that virtually every one of them was often a victim of moods of depression and that they had many anxieties about their own writing. Joseph Conrad used to read Flaubert, and he would feel that there was no use—that he might as well not try to write: after Flaubert, he felt he had nothing to say.

Writing is a lifetime occupation—if one takes it seriously. One lifetime is not too much in which to learn how to write. I would forget about inspiration as the major need of a young writer—that will take care of itself. If you want to write, and think you can, I would look at writing as a series of problems to be solved—problems that can be solved only by hard work and a rigid effort to discipline yourself. I think a young writer should set himself the task of attaining an objective discipline and that he should concern himself as much with the effort to gain a sense of what goes on around him, and of how others think, as with his own moods. In setting this task for oneself, I would look to the stories of Maupassant, Chekhov, and James Joyce's *Dubliners* as models. James Joyce wrote *Dubliners* in his early twenties; these stories are objective studies of people he knew in Dublin. If you will read them, you will see what he observed, what he emphasized, and this should be suggestive to you.

There is one question concerning writing about which no person can give another advice. If anyone asks, should he be a writer, there is no answer. If he wants to be one, and thinks he can be, all the dissuasion in the world will probably not stop him. And if he can't be a writer, probably nothing will make him one. And there is no way in which to find out except by hard work. Writing should be looked upon as hard work, not as inspiration. Confidence in oneself is gained largely through hard work and the gaining of self-discipline. I think it is necessary to build up habits of discipline, to try to be free and honest with oneself in one's perceptions and in one's thinking.

All writers have been influenced by their predecessors; there is no such thing as absolute originality in writing. It is not plagiarism to assimilate influences and to learn from one's predecessors.

I think a young writer should associate with those of his own age who also wish to write. It is better to do this than to try to associate with older writers. Persons your own age meet and face the same problems in their efforts to write that you do. Older persons will be less understanding than you imagine, for they are busy; they have their own problems and their own work. Association with others of your own age who wish to write is very important. You can discuss your mutual problems in such circles much more profitably than you can with older writers. That is the way your own generation will find itself.

Also, I should try to look at objects and environments freshly and I should try to see them as clearly as one can. That is part of learning. Writing is a process of learning and of discovery— self-discovery and discovery of the world. It is an adventure in feeling, in thinking, and in living.

And in writing there are no short cuts. I again state that it is hard work, very hard work if one takes it seriously. A man becomes a writer in a lifetime, not in a day.

Sincerely yours,
JAMES T. FARRELL.

1940

The Language of Hollywood

In America, a tremendous commercial culture has developed as a kind of substitute for a genuinely popular, a genuinely democratic culture, which would re-create and thus communicate how the mass of the people live, how they feel about working, loving, enjoying, suffering, and dying. This culture has become a big business. It is capitalized at hundreds of millions of dollars; it returns many millions in annual profits, rent, and interest; and it employs thousands of men and women to whom it pays additional millions as wages and salaries. At times, the apologists and propagandists for these cultural industries proudly boast of the "cultural" achievements of these industries: on other occasions, however, they assert that these industries produce entertainment, not culture. Let us not quibble over words. The products of these industries (motion pictures, songs, radio plays and soap operas, cartoons, and so on) re-create images of life: they communicate feelings, no matter how banal these may be; they externalize reveries; they fix ideals; they embody and illustrate moral attitudes; they stimulate tastes which in turn create attitudes—in brief, directly and by example, suggestion, innuendo, fable, story, they tell huge masses of people how and what to believe. If the performance of such functions be described as something other than cultural, then the plain meaning of words is being inexcusably debased.

Usually, the debates concerning these industries—and especially the motion picture industry—are concerned with the problem of commercial versus artistic values. Critics of the

164

motion picture industry generally claim that pictures are not artistic enough; their adversaries then reply that pictures are as artistic as they can be made, considering the fact that they must be produced for a profit. The claim that the function of pictures is to produce entertainment serves as a justification of the simple and admitted fact that the fundamental purpose of the motion picture studios is to make money. Not only in motion picture studios, but also in the offices of publishers and theatrical producers, a very common reason for the rejection of many books and scripts is that these do not promise to return a profit. The role of cash value in contemporary American culture is continuously acknowledged on many sides.

All this is common knowledge. It is clear that business considerations play a decisive role in all these fields. And art that we call good, art that we call bad, art that we call counterfeit —all are sold on the commodity market. But today, owing to basic economic causes, something of the most profound significance has happened in American culture: it has been invaded by finance capital. American commercial culture is owned and operated by finance capital.

The motion picture industry clearly illustrates what has happened. Back in 1931 the late Mr. Benjamin Boles Hampton's book, *A History of The Movies* was published; it revealed, as of that date, the change in the economic character of the motion picture industry. As is well known, and as Mr. Hampton clearly described, motion pictures were fathered in peep shows and nickelodeons by a motley crowd of carnival workers, hustling immigrants, and others. This novelty quickly interested the public—and it attracted a lot of nickels. In particular, men with a gambling temperament rushed into this new field in order to exploit it before the novelty wore off. However, it quickly became clear that motion pictures were more than a mere and transient carnivalistic attraction. A golden flood of silver began pouring in. And it was this, and not the cultural possibilities of the medium, that made it so attractive. The stage of novelty did not last long. A period of intense competition followed, punctuated by litigation over patents. The stage of competition led to the formation of a trust, which would standardize trade, control production, eliminate independent producers, and (as Mr. Hampton indicated) mulct the exhibitors.

A bitter struggle ensued between the trust and independents like Zukor and Laemmle. As is usual in the development of a new form of business under capitalism, this struggle was not carried on merely according to laws of competition and in accordance with the due processes of law provided by the courts. There were instances of violence: sluggers were hired, and they smashed cameras, studio, and other tangible assets of more than one independent. In general, the history of the rise of the motion picture industry parallels that of the rise of many other American industries.

The trust was eventually defeated. It was more or less left to die its own death, a process that was related to its conservatism. One of the independents, Mr. Zukor, then rose until he became, perhaps, the most powerful figure in the new industry. This industry expanded rapidly. Movies became increasingly popular. Expenses, salaries, income, all sky-rocketed. This process continued toward the period of the talkies. The money spent, when one reads of it, seems like an orgy. It was paralleled with the boom time and the expenditures of the parvenu stars of that period. Stories and anecdotes of this are common gossip and parlor talk. One director is supposed to have had two stunning and sensational automobiles of a very expensive make and to have gone about Hollywood riding in one and being serenaded from the other by a hired jazz band.

But this period reveals something very important. The so-called normal and natural processes of capitalist competition become one of the fetters on production and expansion if we look at these from the point of view of society. Much waste, duplication and unnecessary costs of production, which are merely a result of the needs of competition, become inevitable. The uneven and continuing process of growth—that is, expansion—leads to more intense and persistent efforts to eliminate the smaller and more economically weak groups or individual entrepreneurs. In this period Mr. Zukor became so powerful in the industry that the federal government even investigated his power. At the same time, each new person, each new group that expanded, that attained power and an important place in the industry, quickly became conservative. Mr. Hampton pointed out that, generally, new capital, and, with it, new figures were needed for each innovation, such as three-reel films, five-reelers and so on. This is a very important fact in the history of the motion picture industry. It suggests how uneven its expansion has been—uneven in the tempo of the development of pictures as an industry, on one hand, and as an art form, a mass cultural medium, on the other. From the very beginning, its attraction was that of the money it promised for those investing in it. At first this money was what many Hollywood persons would now refer to as peanuts, as coffee and doughnuts money. Then it was marked by gambling, speculation, the taking of risks. At this time there was manipulation, competition, maneuvering, struggles for control. This led, further, to the rise of new personalities, the entry of new capital, and to an intensification and extension of the struggle for control, which, in turn, was a struggle for a larger share of profits. This struggle, and the kind of economic expansion it predicated, continuously hampered the technical and artistic development of the motion picture. The feverish irregularity that characterized capitalism as a whole was revealed in the expansion of the motion picture industry. And there is nothing peculiar in the fact that at each innovation those who were powerful would resist change, arguing that innovations would not be good box office. In other words, the public was getting what it wanted, liked what it was getting, and introducing innovations was too risky. But changes were inevitable. The powerfulness of the medium, its potentialities which today are still far from being realized, made innovations inevitable on the technical side; the need for capital to expand made them inevitable on the economic side. By and large, the majority of those who rose in the evolution of the motion picture industry, some of them rising only to fall, were not personages who were seriously interested in culture, experienced in it, anxious to develop a new and great artistic medium. They were speculators, businessmen, gamblers, risk-takers. And the risk-taker of one year soon became the conservative of the next year. In this way, feverishly, irregularly, unevenly, competitively, the motion picture industry expanded until it became a miracle of this century. It grew so big that it could no longer be financed from within. One by one the movie kings went to the bankers. The industry, rising to the billion-dollar stage and becoming one of the most heavily capitalized of American industries, was soon based on huge *blocs* and coagulations of capital: it reached the stage where it was to become dominated by finance capital, where it was to be a virtual monopoly. Economic control passed from the hands of individuals; it resided in the hands of a very few individuals in association with the banks. Entrepreneurs of yesterday were forced out, or else they became managers instead of owners, that is, in the sense in which once they had been owners. This occurred not as a result of dastardly conspiracies but rather as a kind of logical result of the possibilities of this industry and the nature of capitalistic enterprise. The volume of business increased enormously, as we know. The investment in capital kept pace with this increase. The task of financing the industry became such that it was no longer possible for individuals to undertake it. There was nothing to do but call in the banks.

A number of years ago, the French writer, Léon Moussinac, began his book, *Panoramique de Cinema,* by juxtaposing quotations: one from the merchant stating that the film is not merchandise; another from the writer declaring that the film is not art. To the film-maker, it is better to believe, or pretend to believe, that the film be seen as art, to hope that it is art, to gain all the good will he can from prestige that thereby is cast upon films—the glow, the dignity, the respect that is granted to art and culture. To the writer, the character of the work he does, the way he is employed, the continuous manner in which he is blocked from creating as an artist make it indubitably clear to him that the film is merchandise. But the fact is that

the film is both merchandise and art. It is merchandise—a commodity—and it is also an artistic production. It may be good, or
bad, or it may be a fake and a counterfeit, but it is, nevertheless,
an artistic, a cultural production. The contradictions between
the film as merchandise and the film as art are central in the
American motion picture. These contradictions are not general,
formal, abstract. They appear as contradictions concretely, individually, in the making of films; in the give-and-take; in the
conflicts among producers, directors, and writers that often
occur when a film is being made:[1] in general, the results constitute some form of compromise generally weighted on the
side of merchandise. Often this contradiction is concealed by
various apologetic arguments. For instance, Leo C. Rosten, in
his book, *Hollywood: The Movie Colony and the Movie Makers*,
argues that motion pictures are a young industry, an artistic
infant, and that, in consequence, one needs to judge them
artistically with a certain, and at least relative, leniency.
Further, he defends motion pictures by a formal comparison of the film with the printed word and points out how
much rubbish, how much bad art, how much utter verbal
junk is written, printed, and sold. He argues that if you make
such a comparison, the motion picture industry is not alone
to be criticized for its "bad" films, and especially not when
it is further understood that it is an infant art, a child of this
century. Such arguments, such apologetics teach us nothing;
accept them and not only do we understand nothing, but,
worse, we misunderstand everything. The reason so much junk

[1] At the present time I am reading a recent book, *Hollywood Hallucination,* by
Parker Tyler (published by The Creative Age Press, New York, 1944). It is
too late for me to discuss Mr. Tyler's volume in this book, but he has some
illuminating observations to offer on competitiveness as it revealed in the
context of films. He points out that, because of a lack of unity of artistic conceptions, films reveal an inner competitiveness between those involved in the
making of the movies—actors, camera men, costumers, and so on. His observation is just. And he provides many other stimulating insights on the role of the
camera, the character of love in films, and other aspects of the motion picture
in America. I should urge everyone interested in the problems of the motion
picture in this country to read Mr. Tyler's book, for I am confident that it will
—despite difficulties in its style—reward him with fresh and suggestive perceptions.

is produced on a mass scale is because this is *so profitable*. The contradiction between the film as art and the film as merchandise has existed, and has been revealed at every stage of the development of the motion picture industry. Today, because of the size of the industry, and because of the fact that it is now socially organized under a monopolistic aegis, this contradiction can be more clearly, more sharply revealed. With this, the predominating, the almighty, role of the market is nakedly exposed. It is generally admitted that pictures have to make money. They have to make a lot of money. They have to keep making millions of dollars.

At the same time, the motion picture industry has become involved in the whole life of America in innumerable and complicated ways. It touches indirectly on the business life of the nation in a manner that needs to be understood, because this is one of the important specific factors that further focuses and widens this same contradiction. The element of competition in American economy has been heightened, generalized. It is now competition between huge combinations of capital that manufacture and sell different types of commodities. Each of these combinations must jealously guard its product, its good will, prestige, reputation. Indirectly, the motion picture plays an enormous role in causing the sale of various kinds of commodities. It influences styles in dress, in furniture, in the trade and art of the beautician; styles relating to many aspects of the leisure life of, and consumption of goods by, millions of Americans. Trade-marks, business reputations—all these are involved. If a film directly or indirectly endangers a trade-mark, a business reputation, etc., a studio can easily become involved in difficulties—even in expensive litigation—with the producers of the commodity so affected. Not only is the industry owned by the same class that owns all the major means of production of America, but, in addition, it occupies a special place whereby it indirectly affects the increase or decrease of sales of any number of commodities. More broadly, its films touch on the whole religious, political, and social life of America. And as a result of this fact, it is always in danger of becoming involved in difficulties and conflicts. The results of this situation, insofar as they relate to the contradiction between the film as merchandise and the film as art, are incalculable.

The motion picture industry is dominated by a few huge studios; the same is the case in radio. The success of *Reader's Digest* and of the Luce publications reveals the same tendency triumphing in journalism. Some of the consequences of this fact must be noted. It is seemingly paradoxical, but true, that the bigger a corporation producing for the consumer market, the more must it depend on good will. The profits of huge concerns are vitally affected by this fact. Good will, considered as an asset, is highly important. The motion picture industry, which has already revealed in practice how it must expand, demands the widest possible audience. It has something of a mass-production character and a mass audience. And thanks to the stakes involved in the industry, the need for profits and expansion (Hollywood is now on the eve of gaining tremendous control over the world film market), this leads to greater caution. On the whole, there is less willingness to take risks. Capitalism involves risks. But in the stage of finance capital, there is a reduction, a relative standardization, of risk. The greater disinclination to take risks is reflected in the economy of the industry. Its cost of circulation is increased, and because of this the calculations concerning cost of production and concerning profits are affected. Preparations for any "new" venture in films are made long in advance, with an expensive barrage of publicity and fanfare. This fact, in itself, offers eloquent testimony concerning the growing disinclination to take risks.

The star system is also a related and a rather peculiar feature of the social organization of Hollywood. The stars are now virtually walking possibilities of profit. Each major star represents a great asset. As such, he or she must be protected. The protection of stars further demands the reduction of risk. It is financially dangerous to put a star in a role in which he or she may seem unpopular to a considerable section of the audience. This fact has no necessary relationship to the abilities of the stars to play such roles: it is a matter of cold calculation. The element of prestige comes in. In every film in which a star appears, the film must be made according to that star's importance. A star must have expensive directors, expensive writers, and a story that usually is expensive. A star must appear in a film that costs a lot of money. The other actors must not take a film away from the star. This is of vital interest to the star in person; often it is important to the studio. Nowadays, stars, to a certain extent, are "made" by studios. They are trained, coached, treated by beauticians and cosmeticians, nursed and babied along, all at great cost and with the idea in mind that here is an investment that will realize much more than what it costs.

Factors such as these all play their respective roles in (a) the making of profits, (b) in the accumulation of capital and expansion of the market, and, as a consequence of this, (c) in creating the need for so much good will, spread over such a wide human area. Here we see a major reason why the Hollywood studio cannot permit as much freedom in the treatment of a subject as the Broadway producer can, who, in turn, can allow less freedom than the book publisher can. The bigger our cultural industries become, the greater are the restrictions they must impose on the choice and the handling of subject matter. These factors should explain why economic necessities dominate all other considerations. The aims and tastes of the men controlling the industries must be compatible with the economics. One producer may be more sincere, more artistic than another. But all must adjust themselves; all must work within this system.

There can be no doubt that individual taste plays its role in the making of films. What is notable concerning taste is that it is secondary, not decisive. The economic factors more or less map out the boundaries within which individual taste must function, and therefore the role of taste is often reduced to mere detail. Daring, experimentation have a correspondingly similar role. One act of daring experiment and bold honesty may cost a million dollars. Similar risks taken by book publishers can be sustained more easily because the risks are not so great.[2] In addition, those who control the big studios are large-scale capitalists themselves, or they are managers for huge capitalist enterprises. And we have already mentioned, in a direct or indirect way, films touch on all the major economic, political, social, and religious aspects of American life and that the industry needs good will. By representing life on the screen the movies affect every vital material and spiritual interest in American life. There are both objective and subjective interests for doing this. The men in control of the industry have the same class interests as do American capitalists as a whole. They tend to think and act according to their class interests. This is not a matter of dire conspiratorial ideas; it is an inevitable social phenomenon. It is folly to expect them wilfully to produce, and even to lose money on, art that will endanger their basic class interests. Honest art often threatens these interests. This means there is a double restriction imposed on the character of what is produced in motion pictures. Besides promising a profit, a picture must not seriously threaten the class interests of the owners.

Genuine works of art have something new and individual to convey. They reveal new aspects of life, of human feeling. They make us conscious of what hitherto has been hidden, concealed, not clearly grasped in our own consciousness. To assimilate true works of art is often painful, disturbing, difficult; we must make an effort; we must expand our boundaries of feeling and thinking. Growth and assimilation are almost always painful, disturbing, demanding. For we are then forced to change—to alter the force of habit. It is a truism that in a shoddy culture shoddy art generally gains quicker acceptance than does genuine art. The time required for the assimilation of new, more honest, more revealing pictures would be too long, and large losses would have to be sustained during that period. Again we see the role of the element of risk.

Now and then it may happen that a good picture is pro-

[2] It must be noted that the book industry is becoming big business and that a stage of combinations has now been reached.

duced. This is exceptional, often accidental. Usually, bad pictures are produced, and the explanation is as follows: The aim of the studios is to gain a return on investment, to gain profits, rent, and interest. If returns on investment permit the studios to produce great art, then, and *then only*, will they do so; otherwise the artistic values—the truth values embodied in pictures—are, and will remain, merely secondary. In order to be a businessman in this system you must do what business requires; in order to be an artist you must meet the demands and responsibilities required by art. An artist must be sincere, honest, clear, and he must draw on his own inner life and inner tensions for his work. A businessman must stay in business. Q.E.D.!

My analysis can be extended to encompass the economic relationships that play an important role in other fields of culture as well as in the motion picture industry. I use the latter merely as an illustration. Hollywood is not a cause; it is an effect. But the relative purity with which it reveals tendencies now at work in American culture makes it a most illuminating illustration of what I want to convey. The rise of Hollywood to the realm of culture is a phenomenon somewhat analogous to that of the triumph of machine production during the industrial revolution. In the studios many separate crafts and arts are all linked together, mainly under one roof in one serial process. And this requires a large capital investment. This means that we have social methods of artistic creation and of film production carried on for private profits. But those who contribute artistically to this production—with rare exceptions—do not control it. They lose their independence as artists and craftsmen and become employees. Their economic relationship is thereby changed. Most writers, for instance, become wage-working writers. It is true that their wages are generally fantastically higher than those of factory workers, but that is not the decisive factor here. In the economic sense, most writers have a relationship to their employers similar to that of the factory worker to his boss. Just as the worker sells his labor power, so does the writer sell his skill and talent. What he then receives is a wage. All control over the means of his production resides in the employer. Thus, the writer suffers from the same kind of alienation as does the factory worker. He is alienated from control over his means of production, and over what he produces.

And there is a singular character to the alienation of the writer. His real means of production consists of his skill, his feelings, the needs that feed his work, his way of seeing life; in other words, his real means of production is his soul. This is what he sells. As a result of his economic relationships the writer may write what he feels and wants to write only if his employer allows him to do so. But the artist does not determine whether he will or will not do this.

Culture, art, is the most powerful means invented by mankind for preserving the consciousness of civilized man. It externalizes and communicates that which is most important in human life—man's inner life. But in Hollywood the writer who plays the role of the artist, who is ostensibly the creator, sells as a commodity his very ability to create. There is a clear-cut difference between freely creating out of inner need and then selling the creation, and selling the very faculty of creating instead of the results of that creation. The writer may thus write out of his inner self only when his own needs, feelings, and attitudes coincide with the demands of his employer. The nature of these demands has already been uncovered in this analysis. Under such conditions free creation is not a conscious act of will; it is merely accidental, coincidental. Such being the case, it is not accidental, however, that so many Hollywood writers, once they become inured to their work, reveal a retrogression in consciousness. When they write they cannot draw fully on their needs and emotions. Much of their writing is reduced to the level of literary carpentering. They are fettered. And the fettered consciousness must retrogress. This is the real situation. Here we see the mechanism that takes those who should be artists and turns them into mere purveyors of entertainment. Let each make what he can of this situation in accordance with his values, his moral outlook, and with what he wants in life for himself and for his fellow man.

It has already been noted, in passing, that there is a huge capital investment in the distribution end of motion pictures. America—the world, in fact—is almost glutted with motion picture theaters, each of which also must return its profit, its rent, its interest. In many instances these are also organized into chains. Taken together, they constitute a huge and voracious mouth forever crying for commodities to be consumed. And they must be fed. They must stay open; they must have customers continually streaming to the box office. The studios must supply them. Halt this flow of commodities, and bankruptcies will follow. This need, more than any other, conditions the production schedules of the studios. Gigantic blocs of capital are involved in the total structure of the industry. Consequently it must find the widest possible market. This means that the largest possible audience is a necessity. Such an audience can be only a most heterogeneous one, encompassing all age, emotional, and mental levels, and it is only such an audience that will permit this industry to continue. There is no time for costly experiments for educating the tastes of this audience. Staple commodities, based on the lowest common denominator of the mentality and the emotional life of the audience, must be produced. Staple commodities in art, produced in this way, and in order to meet such requirements must mean, in the main, counterfeit art. This is a decisive prerequisite why the masses of the American people really "need" so much Hollywood "entertainment."

Actually, the motion picture industry needs the money of the American masses as much as they need the industry's entertainment. Thus we get an endless barrage of Hollywood publicity and of Hollywood advertising that almost batters the intelligence of the nation into insensibility. Hollywood must do this in order to give the public what Hollywood wants it to want. The audience cannot choose directly. It is not given proper alternatives. Usually it may choose one of various absurd pictures, or none of them at all. When choice is so restricted, it is meaningless to argue that the public really gets what it wants. Also, the contradictions we have observed in the motion picture industry are apparent in American society as a whole. The conditions of American life create alienated and truncated personalities, a fact that has already engaged the attention of more than one generation of sociologists, political scientists, psychologists, judges, social workers, and others. The conditions of earning one's bread in this society create the lonely modern man.

Such conditions help explain the need, sometimes feverish, for an entertainment that so repetitively presents the same reveries, the same daydreams, the same childish fables of success and happiness. So much of the inner life of men is dried up that they tend to become filled with yearnings and to need the consolation of these reveries about people who are happy, healthy, and always successful. Tastes are thus conditioned. Increasingly deprived of proper alternatives from which to choose, the American masses have also become habituated to this taste for the movies. The movies have thereby become a social habit. The kind of culture for profit which we now have would in any case have produced conditions which would aid in the creation of the necessary audience. The two have developed more or less harmoniously. Hence, parallel to the retrogression of consciousness in, say, the Hollywood writer, there is a more widespread and also more pernicious retrogression of consciousness in the motion-picture audience. Social and economic conditions have established the basis for this; the motion picture further enforces it. But such a process cannot continue indefinitely. Eventually a limit must and will be reached. Eventually, there will be a profound revulsion of popular taste. But this will depend not only on the audience being saturated with what it is given; but, more than this, it will depend on fundamental changes that are economic, political, and social in character.

Most motion pictures enervate rather than energize. They distract the masses of the people from becoming more clearly aware of their real needs, their moral, esthetic, and spiritual needs; in other words, the motion pictures of today distract people from the real and most important problems of life. As such, they offer what William James aptly characterized as "a moral holiday." Moral holidays can be refreshing, but when a nation spends so much time on moral holidays, it presents a social problem that must be defined. The gap between the realities of life in our time and the way these are represented on the screen is a wide one. However, the masses of the people do not lose their real needs merely because these are not fulfilled in motion pictures.

It should now be clear that this commercial culture is a safety valve. Here, I offer—in opposition to the conceptions, the apologetics, the theorizations, of such a culture—a different idea of what a culture should do. It should help to create those states of consciousness, of awareness of oneself, of others, and of the world, which aid in making people better, and in preparing them to make the world better. Hollywood films usually have precisely the opposite effect; most of them make people less aware, or else falsely aware. This, to me, is the sense in which Hollywood films fail to fulfill the real cultural needs of the masses of the people. For really to try to satisfy that need, they must not merely envision the masses of the people as they were in the past and as they are now; one must also envision them as they might be; one must establish as a premise their great potentiality. In other words, one must think in terms of the future as well as of the past and of the present. Such a premise is essential if one ideal is a culture that is truly human, a culture that is truly free. Here, in essence, is the great ideal of a free, a human, a socialist, culture which was expressed by Friedrich Engels when he spoke of the possibility of mankind's escaping from the kingdom of necessity and entering the kingdom of freedom.

The content of motion pictures is so familiar to us that it need not be analyzed here in great detail. The values generally emphasized are those of rugged individualism. The lessons inculcated are those implying that the world in which we live, and have lived, is the best of all possible worlds. The dominant characteristics embodied in most motion picture heroes are those of the pioneer, plus those characteristics of the present either consistent with the practices, standards, and the mores of bourgeois America, or else in no vital contradiction to them. The past is re-created in accents of weak nostalgia; the present glorified. The future is promised as no different. All history is, in fact, gradually being revised on the screen until it begins to seem like some glamorous fable. Furthermore, pictures often embody within their very context a kind of visual and illustrative argument indicating that the function of the motion picture is entertainment; thus, the reliance placed on entertainment within the picture, which is itself an entertainment. And although heroes and heroines, on occasion, are given roles, for example, of social workers, which tend to suggest an improvement in the content of motion pictures, the change is merely superficial, and the heroes and heroines remain as absurd as before. Besides, the introduction of social workers as heroes is one indication of how Hollywood really meets social problems. It creates the impression that these problems are soluble by the exercise of individual good will, by babying and nursing the poor, and by eliminating struggle and effort on the part of the poor themselves. Social change is thus treated as purely individualistic. Often, and especially in films dealing with juvenile delinquency, the entire social problem treated is depicted as one caused by pure accident. The absurdity of the heroes and heroines in such films is therefore not the major point on which they should be criticized: the major criticism is that they give totally false impressions of the nature of social problems.

What characterizes almost all Hollywood pictures is their inner emptiness. This is compensated for by an outer impressiveness. Such impressiveness usually takes the form of a truly grandiose Belasco realism. Nothing is spared to make the setting, the costumes, and all of the surface details correct. These efforts help to mask the essential emptiness of the characterizations and the absurdities and trivialities of the plots. The houses look like houses; the streets look like streets; the people look and talk as people do; but they are empty of humanity, credibility, and motivation. Needless to say, the disgraceful censorship code is an important factor in predetermining the content of these pictures. But the code does not disturb the profits, nor does it disturb the entertainment value of the films; it merely helps to prevent them from being credible. The code isn't too heavy a burden for the industry to bear. In addition to the impressiveness of the settings, there is a use of the camera which at times seems magical. But of what human import is all this skill, all this effort, all this energy in the production of effects, when the story, the representation of life, is hollow, stupid, banal, childish? Because masses of people see these films, they are called democratic. In addition, there is often a formal democratic character embodied in the pictures. Common speech is often introduced; an ambassador acts like a regular guy named Joe; poor working girls are heroines, and, now and then, they continue to marry rich men; speeches are introduced propagandistically, in which the common man is praised, democracy is cheered, and the masses are flattered with verbiage. The introduction of such democratic emphases is an additional way of masking the real content of the picture; these emphases are pressed into the service merely to glorify the status quo.

Let us grant that, now and then, an unusual picture is produced—one different from those which I have characterized. Let us not forget that *The Informer* was produced.[3] But can one, or could even ten such films, justify a preponderance of the vastly inferior pictures? One might ask a theologian: if a man steals money, and uses some of it to have masses said for the suffering souls in Purgatory, will he thereby redeem his guilt for theft? To argue that because once in a while we get a picture like *The Informer*, Hollywood is justified, is just about the same as to argue that you should be forgiven for theft because you have used some stolen money for the remission of

[3] I cite *The Informer* rather than a later film for a reason that should be obvious: my overwhelming admiration for this film. It also is an instance, in my opinion, of something more than rare; here, for once, the film was far superior to the novel on which it was based.

punishment, due to sin, of souls in Purgatory. I leave those who argue in this manner to the theologians, who can explain what is wrong with this kind of argument. And, similarly, the argument that bad pictures are necessary to make money which will permit the use of profits for good pictures is a fallacious one. The reason this happens, when it does, is because of the social organization of the industry, and I have already indicated the structure of that.

Hollywood has not created all this counterfeit culture. It borrowed most of what it has given us from tendencies that antedate the appearance of the motion picture on the cultural scene. In fact, other than in the technical realm, Hollywood has invented very little. It has used the powerful inventions of the cinema to repeat most of the cheap stories, the cheap plots, the counterfeits, which have long been printed as stories in commercial magazines. Many of its jokes were familiar even to our fathers, and perhaps our grandparents. Therefore Hollywood is significant mainly because it is a clear-cut example of the development of commercial culture in the period of finance capital. Owing to its size, its wealth, its ability to reach such a mass audience, Hollywood has a penetrating influence in the whole field of culture, one which far exceeds that exerted in the commercial culture it inherited.

Its penetrating influence has long been observed in the drama and in the novel. Hollywood simplifications are introduced more and more into the characterizations of current novels, and this is but one example of the penetrating influences of the motion picture. At present, novels are sold for pictures even before they are written. One can guess what most such books will be like; or, if one wishes to know without trusting to a guess, one can read Louis Bromfield. Another penetrating influence of Hollywood on the novel is the stimulation it has given to a kind of hard-boiled realism that imitates all the manners of serious realistic writing but contains none of the inner meaning, the inner protest against evils, the revelation of the social mechanisms and social structures found in serious realism. This tendency is illustrated by such books as *The Postman Always*

Rings Twice.[4] The influence of the film industry is to be observed, also, in an incalculable way. For instance, there is the diversion of talent, the fettering of talent, in brief, the retrogression in consciousness about which I have already commented. A large proportion of the literary talent of America is now diverted to Hollywood and to radio writing. In many instances there is a certain inevitability in this. For, with the rise of these industries, the writers' situation is such that, on the whole, the book market (except in periods of war prosperity) can support relatively fewer of them. By and large, talent flows toward the highest bidder. A writer represents more than an individual talent; he represents so much social labor that had to be performed in order that he may have developed his talent. This social labor has been expended for the development of literary talent in America. Such talent, instead of returning honest work for the social labor that made its development possible, is used up, burned out, in scenario writing. This is a positive and incalculable social loss. And there can be little doubt of the fact that a correlation exists between the success of this commercial culture and the loss of esthetic and moral vigor in so much contemporary writing. This must be the result when talent is fettered and sold as a commodity, when audiences are doped, and when tastes are confused, and even depraved.

The culture of a society ought not to be viewed as a mere ornament, a pastime, a form of entertainment. It is the life, the consciousness, the conscience of that society. When it fails to serve as such, then it moves farther and farther away from the real roots of life. Such is precisely and unmistakably the situation in America, where we have this tremendous commercial culture spreading itself like an octopus. And consider how many lives, how much labor power, how much talent, how much of social goods is poured not only into Hollywood but

4 An instance that can be cited here is the filming of James M. Cain's book, *Double Indemnity,* where the realism is utterly pointless and unilluminating. To have a suggestion of extra-marital sexual relationships, to have a husband murdered, to have the hero die at the end, and to present this story with touches of vernacular dialogue does not produce *meaningful realism.*

into American commercial culture as a whole. The social cost is fabulous. We are familiar with the news telling us of the financial costs of pictures. A million dollars. More than that. And then we go once again and see what has been produced at such cost. Once again we see a picture so silly that it insults our intelligence. Once again the same old stupid and inept story of boy meets girl, framed, mounted, and glorified until it becomes a monumental absurdity. And so inured are most people to this that they do not even see anything wrong in it.

This entire structure can be metaphorically described as a grandiose Luna Park of capitalism. And if the serious artist enters it, he well may quote these words from Dante: "All hope abandon, ye who enter here."

This is a culture that does not serve men; on the contrary, it makes men its servants. Its highest measure of worth is revealed in little numerals, written in black and red ink on sheets of paper that record profits and losses. Let those who favor this masquerade try to justify it. Far better is it to see it for what it is, and to renounce all the ideals and aims embodied by it. But the writer who does this places himself in that category described by one motion picture executive as "the irresponsible literati." Correct! Irresponsible to this system; responsible to an ideal of trying to show men what life is like now, of seeking to do what one can in the necessary effort of creating in men a consciousness of their problems, their needs, and their future that will help to produce a better society.

1944

More on Hollywood

I

IN THE PAST, the masses of mankind have been the victims not only of class injustices and economic privations but also of cultural scarcity. Even now, liberty of expression and public education are not sufficient to end the reign of cultural scarcity. For the creation of a democratic culture requires that the material, economic, and technical prerequisites for such a culture also be made available to the masses of the people. In the United States these prerequisites do exist, and have long existed. Dr. Horace M. Kallen, in an article, "Of Democracy and the Arts" (*The Journal of Aesthetics and Art Criticism*, Vols. *9-10*), discussed the problem of democracy and culture and pointed out, correctly, the correlation between a culture for the masses and the development and perfection of instruments of communication, which constitute one of the prerequisites for the creation of a democratic culture. Further, Dr. Kallen stated that the movies, one of the arts "addressed to the multitudes," offer real promise for the achievement of this end. Among other reasons for his optimism, Dr. Kallen remarked that "a movie occasionally repeats, and, repeating, transforms, books and plays of larger currency and once in a while draws upon Shakespeare or Dickens. *Whatever else may be said of the movie, it contributes to democratic cultural abundance, bringing within reach of the multitudinous poor much that formerly had had the scarcity-value which established it as an appurtenance of the rich and the privileged.*" (Italics mine.)

Dr. Kallen's hopeful and approving comment on the movies is a logical, but not a *necessary,* deduction of the views on the problem of art and democracy held by the pragmatists, who have been the most consistent expositors in America of the ideas of democracy, of democracy as a way of life. The pragmatists emphasize "shared experience" as the supreme good in life. They see in democracy, more than in any other moral and political system, promise of greater possibilities of this sharing of experience. This ideal of the good emphasizes co-operativeness, getting together. Procedures, instrumentalities, methods of getting people together, for making it possible for them to share experience—these are all good, pregnant with democratic possibilities. In this view, culture must play an educative role. In fact, culture as a process of education is an inescapable conclusion of the premises and postulates of democratic theory.

The pragmatists always have been at their best in discussions of processes and methodology. Dr. Kallen's hopeful impression of the movies has an instrumental emphasis. The movies embody a technique that makes culture for the masses a practical rather than a Utopian ideal. Other pragmatists, too, found cause for feeling as encouraged as Dr. Kallen. For instance, the late George Herbert Mead drew something of the same hopeful emphasis, but in a different context, in his article, "The Nature of an Aesthetic Experience" (*The International Journal of Ethics,* July 26, 1926), in which he described motion pictures as emphasizing escape values that cut "the nerves of action." He characterized the movies as a formal artistic means of objectifying the reveries of the so-called average man. But then, and with particular reference to Charlie Chaplin, he concludes that the arts reaching the American masses, such as the movies, proved that the American was not frustrated in his generous impulses. Then Dr. Mead asserted that, in the movie, as of that time, the American actually lives with his problems rather than escaped from them. Considering the history of the movies from 1926 to the present, one can only say that events have refuted this conclusion by Dr. Mead.

In Mead's work—as well as in John Dewey's—the moral implications of their democratic ideas and the connection between these ideas and their concepts of culture are clear. Along with their overall emphasis on *shared experience* they favor such techniques of communication as will bring out the generous impulses in man, one of which is the so-called esthetic impulse. Herein is embodied what I would unhesitatingly characterize as the best exposition, made from a democratic standpoint, of the solution for resolving the problem of democracy and culture.

But, to repeat, though the material means that permit the solution of this problem have long existed in America, the problem itself has not been solved. On the contrary, the masses have been given a shoddy culture, one which is so shoddy that even its apologists, forced to defend it, can offer only excuses, provisos, and damning admissions. For the sophisticated, for those persons more sensitive and aware, there is a "higher" culture. Problems have often been posed in terms of "high culture" and "low culture," a polarization that is very misleading when related to questions of democracy and culture. Rather than mislead ourselves along this line, it is pertinent to ask point-blank: "Why has America not solved this problem?"

Dr. Kallen qualifies his approval of the movie when he says: "*Whatever else may be said of the movie* . . ." (My italics.) Furthermore, in the same article, he writes: "Of course, printing press, post office, phonograph, camera, radio, are neither monopolies of the democracies nor can they be permitted by democracies to become monopolies. . ." More important than occasional presentations of Shakespeare on the screen, than occasional "good" movies, there is this formulation: "Whatever else may be said . . ." That is precisely what needs to be investigated. In my earlier article, "The Language of Hollywood," I attempted to get at some of the features of this "Whatever else . . ." and in it indicated that what must not be allowed to happen, according to Dr. Kallen, is happening. Briefly, the camera is becoming a monopoly.

The social organization of the movies militates against the achievement of a democratic culture; instead, there has been created a mere culture of merchandise. With this fact in mind, a final remark is required at this point.

Failure to understand always exacts its penalties, and this failure on the part of the pragmatists is now exacting penalties. They continue to speak in terms of hopes, whereas the class realities of American society render their hopes Utopian. Again, any serious analysis of these problems *must* explain Dr. Kallen's "Whatever else." His very formula here is very suggestive. Dr. Kallen's superiority to most of those who write on the movies and see great promise in them, his opinion is based on the precise formula of apologetics. That is why I have dealt with it in detail here. Nothing that can be strongly defended needs to be explained in the "whatever else may be said" formula. But again and again in writings on the movies it is this kind of defense that is used.

In contrast to the remarks of Dr. Kallen, it will be well to listen to the words of a responsible and highly successful Hollywood executive, Mr. Darryl F. Zanuck. In 1943, a Writers Congress was held in Hollywood under the auspices of the University of California and the Hollywood Writers Mobilization. I omit discussion of many passages from the speeches that could be quoted, and also a discussion of the declaration of independence, drawn up by those who participated, in the name of literary freedom, and so on. The reader can well be spared the easy irony that could be suggested by this document. Here, let us concentrate merely on the paper read by Mr. Zanuck to the assemblage and later published in *The Saturday Review of Literature* (October 30, 1943) under the title of "Do Writers Know Hollywood?" This article carries the subtitle "The Message Cannot Overwhelm the Technique." (Incidentally, the paper does not contain even one illuminating sentence on technique.) At all events, here is a statement of what a responsible producer thinks. After explaining that different types of pictures are made in cycles, he said: ". . . the profit motive in the final analysis has determined our course. That is true, but like so many other generalizations, it is only partly true. [???] Certainly, the producer must have the element of profit constantly

before him. In the circumstances, it cannot be otherwise. . . .
We have radiated sweetness and light since the advent of pictures, and we have carefully refrained, for the most part, from
even remote contact with the grim and pressing realities before
us in the world." [1] Now there are stirrings, "a dawning recognition of the facts of life." During the general period of Hollywood's almost fabulous growth there were two World Wars,
many revolutions, civil wars, and an assorted variety of minor
and less-than-world wars. Whenever there was a respite from
wars and revolutions, there was, as Marx put it, "the peaceful
warfare of competition." Thousands of men and women of
various professions and from all over the world raised voice on
voice, cry on cry, because of injustice, misery, agony, unhappi-
ness. At last, with all that has happened in our own lifetime, the
picture-makers now reveal "stirrings of late—a dawning recognition of the facts of life." Progress has been achieved. And this
dawning recognition of the facts of life is Mr. Zanuck's answer
to the critics who accuse the movies of "commercialism." What
has caused this new dawn over Hollywood, Glendale, Burbank,
and Beverly Hills, California? "Is it possible to make pictures
which have purpose and significance and yet show a proper
[this raises a problem of definition] return to the box office?
I believe it is. I believe the answer is entertainment." [2]

Ergo: if you can put the facts of life into a film entertainingly and make a "proper" profit, then you have the material
conditions which justify the film-makers in their discovery of
the facts of life. But this is crucial in Mr. Zanuck's view: Enter-

[1] This is not completely true. Mr. Zanuck says that it is true "for the most part."
In the past, one or another Hollywood studio has made a film about "the grim
realities." It is well to call attention to one such film, a product of the depression—*Gabriel Over The White House*. This was a reactionary film which
"solved" the crisis of the early 1930's by a virtual dictator in the White House,
a big navy, and so on. At the time, radicals and liberals attacked it, including
some who see signs of great "progress" in Hollywood—now that there is a
different Stalinist line in operation.
[2] The argument about entertainment is not new. It is merely a euphemistic repetition of the argument about giving the public what it wants. *History of the
Movies,* by Benjamin Boles Hampton, which I mentioned in "The Language of
Hollywood," justified the film industry against earlier critics on the ground that
it provided entertainment and gave the public what it wants.

tainment is essential in order that serious, worth-while stuff be made "palatable." The motion picture audience—"the run-of-the-mill patron"—Mr. Zanuck believes, has been ready for palatable entertainment and pictures about the facts of life, and with a purpose, for many years. But—"We simply have failed to dress such pictures properly. It is a gap we must bridge in order to justify our place in the social, economic, and political scheme of things."

In addition, Mr. Zanuck discusses the films *The Ox-Bow Incident* and *Watch On The Rhine*, both of them pictures with a purpose—that is, art. But *The Ox-Bow Incident*, which drew badly, was a "failure," for "unless we can get it before as wide an audience as sees the average good picture which has no purpose but to divert," it does not get its message across to enough people. This is why "box office counts, not because it determines profits, which are important, but because we fail unlesss we can get a maximum turnout for these pictures which guide and enlighten the public. *Watch On The Rhine* was a success. Why? It was 'a marvelous piece of visual entertainment.' Although its theme hits hard, 'the pure entertainment values are supreme.' This is an ideal example of sugar-coating the pill." It seems that the sugar-coating consists of the fact that "the personal elements appear to predominate." All in all, this film was "an adroit package." Is further comment here necessary?

Now that Hollywood—forever so magical—has discovered the processes of artistic alchemy whereby the facts of life are put into a sugar-coated pill and wrapped up in an "adroit package"—what is, what should be the purpose of films? Films should channel, organize thought in favor of a world without war, declares Mr. Zanuck. "It is up to us to help give . . . substance and reality" to such thoughts. Can films achieve this? Yes, for "We have the talent, the know-how."

One need only hastily glance through the daily newspapers to realize the urgency of this need. Nonetheless, in achieving the purpose which, according to Mr. Zanuck, will justify Hollywood in the scheme of things, "We've got to start gradually."

We can make the point that *so desperately needs making today, but we must do it entertainingly.*" (Italics mine.) This is where the writer comes in. It is up to him "to find the means and the method by which pictures of meaning, of significance can be made enjoyable to the mass of the people."

Mr. Zanuck also spoke of *Wilson*, which, I believe, was then in process of production. "The film will cost $3,000,000." Coupling it with Wendell Willkie's *One World* (purchased by Twentieth Century-Fox Film Corporation but not as yet produced), he said that unless these then-projected films "are seen by the biggest possible number of people, we will have failed in making them. Just getting our money out of them or even making a profit is beside the point. These pictures, I feel, have something of importance to say to the world. They cannot say it if people do not see them in great numbers. [Why?] I can tell you that unless these two pictures are successful from every standpoint, I'll never make another film without Betty Grable in the cast." [3]

At all events, Mr. Zanuck affirmed his readiness to "forge ahead" and produce films without Miss Grable, to "break new trails," to play his "part in the solution of the problems that torture the world." But he set one condition on his fulfillment of this task. The world must go to cinemas and see the films he produces. If the world—that is, a sufficient number of millions of its inhabitants—should not go to see the entertaining films Mr. Zanuck was planning, then it would have to continue to suffer the tortures of the facts of life and the dangers of World War III. Mr. Zanuck would then give it only films starring Betty Grable. It is not possible for Mr. Zanuck to help achieve everlasting peace unless the films he produces, in dedication to this effort, are "successful from every standpoint." Then he concluded his address by calling on writers "to lead the way." And as for them— ". . . if they have something worthwhile to say, let them dress it in the glittering robes of entertainment and they will find a *ready market.* (Italics in original.) No

---

[3] I make no effort to interpret the meaning of this reference to Miss Betty Grable. Let each interpret it as he is inclined to.

producer who is worthy of the name will reject entertainment, and without entertainment no propaganda film is worth a dime."

II

By contrasting the views of Dr. Kallen and Mr. Zanuck we can see in a sharper and more direct light the contradiction I have already mentioned. Dr. Kallen is a philosopher who has tried theoretically to forge a perspective and vision of the ideals of democratic individualism. Mr. Zanuck is a product of the society about which Dr. Kallen has written. In a sense, he has been an individualist in action. Damon Runyon and others refer to him as a great American. Mr. Zanuck's career in the motion picture industry is a Horatio Alger story. While Dr. Kallen deals with the possibilities of the motion picture as a medium that can end cultural scarcity, Mr. Zanuck talks about the conditions on the basis of which he will produce serious films. What separates the theoretician and philosopher and the practical business man of culture? The answer is simple: *Box office.*

Here box office cryptically indicates the facts of class society based on the ownership of the means of production. These facts, which, incidentally, are related not solely to the motion picture industry, explain why people are kept apart, why there does not exist that real sharing of experiences that is emphasized—and properly so—in the writings of the pragmatists. Various pragmatists often stress techniques of co-operation and communication that will heal and eliminate conflict, that will get people together. In a sense, but not in the precise and full sense that a philosopher like John Dewey really means it, the movies have become such a technique. But they perform this role on the principle of justifying and glorifying the status quo. And as I have already noted, this causes a retrogression of consciousness. The tendencies revealed by the movies in such a blatant form indicate why America has not solved the problem of democracy and culture.

In this context, a further observation on Mr. Zanuck's speech is enlightening. Throughout his speech, Mr. Zanuck emphasizes words like *we*, meaning those persons in the motion picture industry like himself. These are the persons who are going to emphasize the correct ideals. They are going to bring messages to the masses of the people. The "run-of-the-mill patron" of motion picture theaters is merely to be ready to receive messages. Briefly, Mr. Zanuck talks like a man of authority. In the clearing of these new paths he assigns roles to be performed, just as though he were casting for a film. And his own part is made clear, for he tells us what he will do. A role is to be assigned to writers—they will cook up facts and sugar-coat messages. And he assigns a role to the masses of the people. They will swallow—at an admission fee. In "The Language of Hollywood" I remarked that when choices are restricted, it is meaningless to argue that the public really gets what it wants, for no genuine alternative is offered. This statement is unwittingly confirmed by Mr. Zanuck's speech.

The substance of Mr. Zanuck's remarks can be boiled down to the premise that in the motion picture industry the market is the controlling factor. There can be no other interpretation of Mr. Zanuck's remarks regarding this point. My knowledge of him is restricted to what I have read by and about him, but on the basis of such restricted knowledge I would most definitely assert that he is not a stupid man. Withal, a strict and literal interpretation of his speech could well imply such a conclusion. What serious person in the whole history of mankind has ever argued that in order to bring light to a darkened world, in order to assuage the tortures of mankind in a period of the most terrible war in history, it is necessary to entertain? Taken literally, such a remark is almost inconceivable. Could any real teacher, moralist, political thinker, honestly say that? Did Jesus Christ and the Twelve Apostles believe that in order to spread the Gospels they had to do so with entertainment? Did Christ have Mary Magdalene perform fan dances or sing songs or entertain before He preached? The fact is that when you really teach, you do not need to entertain in the Hollywood sense of entertainment. The fact is that when you have an imperative message to give, you do not plan a set of conditions for delivering it. You do not declare that unless the S.R.O. sign is put out your message has failed and that here you will not deliver it again. All this is a truism. But the glaring light it casts on Hollywood, and on the social system of which Hollywood is an expression, is its own damning comment. It is to such a pass that we have come, thanks to the almighty power of cash value.

The fact, then, that Hollywood pictures do not truly provide for the spiritual, moral, and esthetic needs of the masses of the people can be expressed in the difference between what the motion picture could be and what it is. No other art medium has the power, the potentiality, or the future of motion pictures. This is recognized by everyone. I doubt if any man of this century was more sensitive to, more aware of, more concerned with, the cultural needs of the masses than was Lenin. He recognized the incalculable cultural potentialities of the motion picture. Anyone aware of the cultural problems must recognize these potentialities. No cultural medium invented by man could do as much to free mankind, to lift the level of consciousness of the human race to the same extent as the motion picture. But the fact is that, far from raising that level, it lowers it and causes stagnation. Mr. Zanuck's speech documents this fact. He tells us that motion picture people have the talents, have what he calls "the know-how." This is indisputable. And whenever a Hollywood studio does not have on its payroll the particular person needed to contribute anything necessary for the success of a film, it usually can hire such a person, regardless of cost. The talent of America, of the world, can be bought by Hollywood. The industry has the skill and the material resources to do almost anything it wants to do. If it fails, what is the reason? If that reason is not basically economic, what can it be? Thus, consider another of Mr. Zanuck's admissions. He said in 1943 that only then was Hollywood discovering the facts of life, insofar as the content of films was concerned. In Leo C. Rosten's book, *Hollywood*, there is a table of the production costs of Hollywood biennially from 1921 to 1937. These, as given by Mr. Rosten, were:

1921	$ 77,397,000
1923	86,418,000
1925	93,636,000
1927	134,343,000
1929	184,102,000
1931	154,436,000
1933	119,343,000
1935	161,865,000
1937	197,741,000

Add these figures. They total $1,229,281,000. This fantastic sum is only part of Hollywood's cost of production over a period of less than twenty years. On the basis of these figures it can be said that the motion picture industry spent, in total costs of production, more than one billion, two hundred and twenty-nine million, two hundred and eighty-one thousand dollars before its leading executives, its most talented and able persons, by their own admission, began to discover, with even the slightest pretense of seriousness, what are called the facts of life. According to another table provided by Mr. Rosten (who is friendly to the industry and really defends it), six Hollywood studios in 1938 produced 251 films, the production of each of which cost a quarter of a million dollars or more. This also was in the Zanuck pre-facts-of-life era.

Assume that the dead past is buried. At all events, the new era has dawned in pictures. Hollywood has discovered social consciousness (plus entertainment), propaganda (plus entertainment), ideas (plus entertainment). Mr. Zanuck spoke of his film, *Wilson*. It has since been released, and is supposed to be a smash hit. Mr. Zanuck, therefore, can continue to produce films without Betty Grable and not break his promise. According to his advance announcement, *Wilson* was to cost three million dollars. It may have cost a little more, a little less; at any rate, its cost, as the boys say, isn't peanuts. It has been widely hailed as a successful film which demonstrated how Hollywood has now proven that it can produce *serious* films. And because many critics and others have cited it as a new and important departure in American films, an analysis of this picture is pertinent.

First of all, Mr. Zanuck and others involved in making this film did not neglect entertainment values. According to publicity about the film, eighty-seven "beloved songs" are played or sung in it. Not only must one listen to them while one sits waiting for the "message," but one must listen to a band (variously costumed according to scene) at the risk of having one's eardrums shattered. Here is neither a sugar-coated pill nor an adroit package; no, here is noise. At times the band becomes so noisy that history is drowned out. All that is missing, from the standpoint of entertainment, is Miss Betty Grable, appearing, properly clad, in the final scene and singing a song, which might have been specially written and composed for this film and titled, "History Is Just an Oldtime Song." In fact, there is so much entertainment in *Wilson* that one wonders whether it is an historical film or a musical show. Woodrow Wilson—in this Hollywood version of him—was a man who needed entertainment every bit as much as the American public. And he gets it: football, baseball, vaudeville, classical music, popular songs. And when the film Wilson is not being entertained by others, he and his family sing *Put On Your Old Gray Bonnet* and *By the Light of the Silvery Moon*. No, not even the processes of history can be unfolded without entertainment. No chance for songs and bands is missed.

The film Wilson is singularly devoid of personal characterizing attributes, of personal relationships, of temperament and psychology. He bears the same name as the historic Woodrow Wilson, is involved in the same events, and more or less looks like that real Wilson. The portrayal scarcely goes further. The real Woodrow Wilson was a man of temperament, even though that temperament may have been concealed somewhat by a haughty manner. He was a man of contradictions, contradictions indicative of inner conflicts and doubts. As John Maynard Keynes remarked in *The Economic Consequences of the Peace*,

Wilson's temperament was neither that of a student or scholar, but of a clergyman. He was aloof, rather lonely, and often expressed his haughtiness by a refusal to brook any proposal, suggestion, or criticism if these involved any reflection on him personally. Many of his traits suggest a man guarding his own personality, his own sense of himself. He was often vacillating and would put off decisions and actions until the last moment. Keynes, at Versailles, was definitely surprised to discover that Wilson had thought nothing through. On the level of culture and responsiveness, he was the inferior of Balfour and Clemenceau (again to agree with Keynes) and in political abilities, as these relate to the conference table, he was no match for Lloyd George. Stubborn and inflexible, he often stimulated opposition and disagreement. But his stubbornness and inflexibility were not accompanied by real determination and doggedness. He was deficient in will, and this was substituted for by his facile capacity to justify himself in moral and self-righteous utterances. One of his major contributions to a torn and agonized world consisted of parochial letters, compounded from such elements as stylistic derivations from Burke and the spirit of parish morality. He was distinctly lacking in originality of mind, and Keynes's remark to the effect that Wilson had thought nothing through is distinctly justified by a scrutiny of his papers, his career, and the memoirs and other writings of those who knew him. His political ideas, as these are now lauded in legend, expressed by him with a certain formal nicety and formal political harmoniousness, were common ones of his era. The idea of a League of Nations can be found implied or variously expressed in his time.

The fact that Wilson's ideas were not original, however, is not a necessarily derogatory criticism of him. But it is to be noted, in respect to the Wilson legend, that he was deficient in his grasp of practical matters. His shrewdness enabled him to put into effect some of the demands of his adversaries; for instance, those of Theodore Roosevelt. His formal views were democratic and clothed in democratic language; in personal matters, however, he was inclined to be authoritative.

It is no secret that he resisted advice and consultation at Versailles and that his manner of doing so offended his collaborators. At many points in his career he hesitated in reaching decisions, and it seems that at such times he was pulled in opposite directions by inner conflicts and doubts. Like him or dislike him, it is clear that Wilson was a man of complex temperament, inner conflicts, contradictory personal traits.

There is none of this in the film *Wilson*. Hollywood's Woodrow Wilson is a synthetic composition. On one hand, he is a prototype of the typical middle-class American. As such, he is a man of sentiment and nostalgia; he sings sentimental songs with his family. He is teased by his daughters and his wife. He goes to baseball and football games, vaudeville shows, and so on. At the same time, he is a leader of almost superhuman wisdom: he is always right; his is the vision that will save humanity. His wisdom and vision are brought out by speeches made in private as well as in public.

It is impossible to discuss any artistic representation of Woodrow Wilson without referring to historical facts. Lost in a display of irrelevant entertainment, newsreel clips, and the like, there is, in the film, a very simple interpretation of the First World War. As presented, that war was a conflict of good and evil, with German militarism the sole evil, instead of merely one of several evils. In other words, the film substitutes a simplified moralistic interpretation of that war for a historic and economic one. Of course, this interpretation is very popular now, during the present war, and those who disagree with it are called names. But the facts of history remain nonetheless, recorded in many volumes of historiography. The best historical research on the background and originals of the First World War was done in the United States, by scholars such as Sidney Bradshaw Fay and Harry Elmer Barnes. C. Hartley Grattan's *Why We Fought* cites the record irrefutably. The diplomatic papers, the letters and diaries of ambassadors and statesmen, the secret treaties, the Versailles peaces—all are ignored by those who would impose on us the simplified explanation that the cause of World War I was a conflict between good and evil. Such conflicts are much simpler than world wars for steel and gold, wars for boundaries, markets, and raw materials. In the film, all the intricate background of the First World War is omitted. Furthermore, we have a villain named Lodge, and the failure of Mr. Wilson is explained as the result of a personal feud between him and Senator Lodge. This rivalry is purely personalized and stereotyped; what these men really represented is either omitted or confused. In brief, history is unfolded before our eyes without any real indication of forces or tendencies. And, in passing, the rivals of Mr. Wilson in the Senate, a "little group of willful men," represent no one but themselves. Actually, this famous remark was really uttered by Wilson in reference to the six Senators—among them Robert M. LaFollette and the late Senators Norris and Lane—who attempted a filibuster in order to block the bill proposing the arming of American merchant ships prior to the entry of the United States into the war in April, 1917. The point about the Senators who fought the Versailles Treaty is that they did voice the sentiments of many groups in America, among them, the farmers. And such a statement of history as the film presents only confuses, misleads.

Now, no one denies that the producers of a historic film—like the novelist—have the right to select; in fact, they must be selective. It would be absurd to demand that *Wilson* embody the whole history of its period. But the selection here is very arbitrary and creates a false version of events. This leaves it open to criticism both from the standpoint of history and of drama. A scholar with any pride and integrity in his reputation could scarcely recommend this film.

The life of Woodrow Wilson was the focus of a great historical tragedy. Never before had the hopes of so many millions of human beings been placed in one leader as was the case in Wilson's life when he went to the Peace Conference. Regardless of reasons, there was failure, tragedy. This failure, this tragedy is not merely personal; it is historic. The conflicts, the disagreements at Versailles are indicative of the clash of historic forces and interests, of differences in human aims, hopes, desires. The men at that Conference dealt with the fate of millions—of humanity itself. The differences in personalities, levels of culture, temperaments, and aims of the Big Four were merely the dramatic focus of more important differences. What drama here! Drama, moreover, that can be rendered by the motion picture more effectively than by any other medium. Consider this drama, the tension it reveals, and then consider the treatment of Versailles in *Wilson*. Mere rhetoric, mere formality. In the film there is not even an iota of genuine drama.

Was Woodrow Wilson's life tragic in the Aristotelian sense? Let others debate this. Here it is important merely to remark that in the film the historic aspects of the tragedy are sacrificed, and only the personal experience of a single man is presented. The agony of humanity is reduced solely to the defeat, suffering, the breakdown of Woodrow Wilson. The simplification of theme is synthesized with the simplification of the tragedy.

There was tension in the real Woodrow Wilson; there is no tension in the Wilson of the film. Just as the collapse of Wilson is not prepared for in the film, neither is the historic significance of Wilson's failure illuminated. Thus we can see the nature of the substitution of the personal tragedy for the historic one. Here is a lesson in Hollywood dramaturgy. Here are parts of the mechanics of that dramaturgy. It is a dramaturgy that relies on artificial synthesis. Thus, the film's Wilson is a "regular" American with sentimentalities that are supposed to be sentiments; he is also a leader who is always right, a veritable Messiah. But the Messiah is as human as you or I. He likes what we like. His personal life is like ours. The personal and the official are synthesized so that the historic is as simple as the personal.

Further, this film substitutes motions, gestures, sentimentalities for *relationships*. The film's Wilson has no *real* and human relationships. How different from the real Woodrow Wilson! For let us not forget that his aloofness with others in itself is indicative of one type of human relationship. In the film, Colonel House is like a supernumerary. To indulge in a bad pun, House is merely in the house. He is present when the first Mrs. Wilson dies; he is seen returning from Europe to report to

Wilson. But what he says is not revealed to us. This is obviously less important than the bands.

Or take Tumulty. In the film he is a breathless Jimmie Higgins with messages to deliver. Again no genuine relationship is portrayed. Or Wilson and the members of his Cabinet! Unless one is very attentive, one will miss seeing them. Nor is Wilson ever shown as Commander in Chief of millions in a World War. It obviously would have been impossible to reveal all of Woodrow Wilson's personal and political relationships; but in the film *none* is re-created. In politics, the personalities of men are almost nakedly exposed. This is not the case, however, in the film. For here there is a formal synthesis of the private and the political, and it is neither private nor political. Here, a drama, a tragedy of Shakespearean proportions is turned into almost a semi-musical show.

In theory, democracy is a form of government in which final authority is lodged in the people; in theory, the people rule. Here, however, is a democratic film in which the people are supernumeraries and the leaders the chief characters. And in this representation, consider the taste revealed. Expensive and grandiose decorations in technicolor; shots of the White House suggestive of luxury, of fine textures and comfortable living. The man of democracy, Woodrow Wilson, has a wedding fit for kings, with diplomats in uniforms with medals, and lovely ladies in beautiful and probably specially designed dresses. Or, there is a White House reception. And, of course, there is entertainment at this.

But while the man Woodrow Wilson is a "regular" (read Hollywood) American in the film, he is also a man who likes high Culture. The entertainment at the White House is "high" culture—classical music. Ladies in lovely evening gowns and men in tails—representative of Senators, diplomats, and others among the great who are admissible into the tents of the mighty —drink coffee from demi-tasse cups, eat delicate tidbits, and talk about democracy—democracy and a war for democracy.

In contrast—how is the First World War treated? Leaving aside Wilson, it is hastily included in newsreels, clips of Hollywood stars selling Liberty Bonds, of farmerettes, and so on. The film was really written and produced from the standpoint of those who give orders. Its real, but undoubtedly unwitting, perspective, can be symbolized as an office desk. History, politics, democracy, mankind— all are seen from above. One can look at it from more than one standpoint, regard it in terms of various relevant questions asked, but nonetheless the character and quality of the film creeps out. It is a film about democracy which is discussed by men in tails and silk hats. Its hero is a man who reveals democracy in speeches. And singularly, the Wilson of the film is a man who is constantly giving orders or issuing pronunciamentos.

But while one notes all these aspects of *Wilson,* the picture shows a remarkable verisimilitude in many matters of small detail. The characters look quite like the historic personages they portray. Even if a historic figure appears for as little as five or ten seconds, obviously, great pains were taken to make the actor look like the person he characterizes. The details of chronology are irrefutable. In 1912, Woodrow Wilson was nominated at Baltimore; so it is in the film. In the film, the real and the fictional are synthesized—fictional scenes and newsreels. Details of set, scene, this is all extraordinary because of the illusion of reality that is created. The technique used is parallel to that of another film with a message—*Mission to Moscow.*[4] Professor Meyer Schapiro analyzed this technique in a review of *Mission to Moscow* printed in *Partisan Review* (May-June, 1943). I quote: ". . . the historical and political content of the film should also be considered from another angle, as a type of propaganda film new to this country. The events leading up to the war are presented at the same time as the headlined history familiar to newspaper readers and also as the personal experiences of an official eye-witness and participant. Through the combination of newsreels of Hitler Germany and Stalin Russia with the re-enacted story of Mr. Davies, the latter takes on the qualities of an authentic historical reality . . . the spec-

[4] An editor of a motion picture magazine remarked to me that some persons in Hollywood have said that *Mission to Moscow* made *Wilson* possible.

tator feels himself transported behind the scenes to enjoy the
same direct contact with the secret historical process as in his
contemplation of the public review of the Nazi army." The
sense of the actual events being set before one's eyes is created
in *Wilson* in a way very similar to that in *Mission to Moscow*.
To quote Professor Schapiro further: "The sentiment of the
little man of the democracies that world politics are a mysteri-
ous game in which figures beyond his own plane of vision
manipulate the fate of the world for motives which are never
quite clear is dissolved by the omnipresence of a plain-spoken
American, who moves about everywhere armed with the wonderful authority of a mission from the President . . ." In
Wilson, this character is the President.

And again: The President plays golf, he sings sentimental
songs, and his speeches, because of the times we live in, have the
ring of what is familiar to newspaper readers and the radio
listeners. Further, the public is familiar with the noise, the
shouting, the hot dogs and the bands that are part of the picture of a political convention, and this is pieced together with
what is assumedly the inside story. The secret springs of history
are revealed, and in connection with that revelation, in order to
humanize it, we have the entertainment values—the eighty or
more songs, the bands, and the family songfest. History is
domesticated. In this context consider the scene where Wilson
learns of his first nomination: Joe Tumulty rushes to see Wilson—on the golf course; [5] Wilson is seen as an obviously unam-
bitious person whose personal emotions are not roused by the
chance to become president, and at the same time we gain a
glimpse of the private life of a great man. A band suddenly
appears—thanks to Tumulty—and plays. The secret springs of
history and the private lives of historical personalities are presented in this way. And it is all humanized by "entertainment
values."

Professor Schapiro further wrote: "Outside . . . two poles
of the human and the superhuman . . . lie all those treacher-

[5] In *Mission to Moscow* Joe Davies receives the great call while he is on a
fishing trip.

ous, mediocre, ignorant and foolish elements who dare to question the wisdom of the great leaders . . ." The same can be said of *Wilson*. Wilson of the film is the great leader, at once human and superhuman; he is the man who possessed the true vision of the future; he is, also, questioned by the foolish and the mediocre, not to mention Congressmen and Senators. This suggests a special clue on the way as to how we should interpret historic facts. According to this domesticated pictorialization of history, there was a man who knew just what had to be done. The simple, the malevolent questioned him. The synthesis of history in newsreel and fictional scenes creates the illusion of unquestionable veracity; and verisimilitude of detail adds to the illusion. Then, what the average member of the audience remembers of history from what he has been told in newspapers and on the radio comes to the rescue of film-makers. The agonizing history of twentieth-century man thus bears witness to the message expressed by the leader. Newsreels, newspaper headlines, plus the pictorialization of historic figures with convincing accuracy, all present history as the average man can grasp it—in newspapers and in theaters. In addition, the speeches made by the leader, even in private, are formal: they sound like the radio speeches of a leader. The average man also comes in contact with history by listening to the speeches of political leaders over the radio. All this—*let me stress*—heightens the illusion of reality in the fictionized parts of the film. This in turn helps to give an overpowering credibility to the message. The grossness, simplification, and exceedingly special "selective emphasis" of the film is hereby made to seem overpoweringly real.

In terms of serious dramaturgy, all this is to be attacked, exposed, condemned, even though it is brilliantly done—brilliantly executed as a means of "getting something across." Mr. Zanuck, as we have already learned, boasted that men in the film industry have "the know-how." At this point, we can confirm that statement. There is, I repeat, real "know-how" in *Wilson*. But insofar as all this skill is concerned, the history books and documents exist in vain.

Professor Schapiro also connected the technique of *Mission to Moscow* with Siegfried Kracauer's book, *Propaganda and the Nazi Film,* published by the Museum of Modern Art (and Mr. Kracauer is an expert on the German film). This work contains a brilliant account and analysis of the technique of the Nazi film. The author discloses how the irrefutable, the facts of history, the newsreels, maps and statistics, are introduced in Nazi films, and how these create "a deceitful pseudo-reality." Such a technique helps convey to members of the audience the sense that they have directly experienced history. Music and song are further used as a means of lulling or stirring the audience. And the official version of events is added. The real and the official are thereby linked. The official becomes, for many of the lulled audience, the real. It was Mr. Kracauer's conclusion that this technique was peculiar to the films of a totalitarian nation such as Hitler's Germany; but the parallels in this technique as used in Nazi films and American films, about and with a mission, such as *Mission to Moscow* and *Wilson,* indicate that it is not indigenous to Nazi Germany. As Professor Schapiro remarks, it "seems to arise naturally from the needs of the modern state, which operates on two planes and possesses a double set of truths, one the practical knowledge which governs the action in the interests of the ruling groups, the other the official doctrines and justifications addressed to the mass of the people who have little voice in the state and are the victims of the crises and wars that follow."

In films where this technique is employed, in films of such an official character, democratic forms must be empty. It is impossible to present a picture of this kind and to reveal democratic forms in operation in any live or real sense. To do the latter would expose the nature of the film. Thus, the passive character of the masses in *Wilson.* They are talked to, talked to directly in the film and in the theater, by the wise and good leader who represents them, officially, in the pattern of events that are filmed. Thus democracy is reduced to speeches of the leader. As already pointed out, this is the function of the speeches that Wilson makes in the film.

Films embodying this technique to a greater or lesser degree can only treat democratic forms as empty. It is impossible, in fact, to produce a film like this and reveal democratic forms in any other light. The masses are addressed in speeches. This overlaps into the leader—the actor here—speaking out of the film to the audience itself, which is also a part of the masses of the people. Thus there is a meaning to the fact that the film Wilson talks with such formality even in private, using the language of public speech in his meetings—vis-à-vis others, including friends. The official nature of the film demands that the portrait of the leader be an officialized one. He is characterized not as a man of temperament and inner tension; he is characterized throughout, even in private, as an official.

Humanization is achieved only by his interest in entertainment, and so on. In this respect, it may be noted that when the characterization of Wilson changes in the film from the official and leader to that of human being, Wilson becomes an average man who shares the tastes of average men—that is, tastes selected in the writing of the film—and he, too, becomes passive. Further, there is an added, if small, detail to be noted here. In minor scenes there is often an episode between the leader and a servant—and the servant is a common stereotype. Furthermore, such a scene is emphasized more than one which shows the official really at work. In such a film the servants are usually more prominent than are the secretaries.

Now an added interpretation of entertainment values can be offered. The formal entertainment lulls the mind, softens the critical faculties, deadens the sense of reality. Many of the songs in Wilson are old-time popular songs that awaken old memories. They stir nostalgias that have a distracting effect, putting many of the spectators into a wistful good humor. The audience thereby becomes more receptive. Outside the theater there is a cold, everyday world of war and drudgery and sadness. War threatens to ruin that world. Inside, here is an explanation of how and why that world is threatened, and here is a hero who can—if only he is listened to and followed—save one, lead one. And along with this lesson there is a warmth of soothing sentimentality. The entertainment values play a functional role.

They blur; they anesthetize the audience so that it becomes all the more easy for it to accept as reality the grossness and over-simplification of the story.

Here, then is an advanced development in the current motion picture. But such films as *Wilson* and *Mission to Moscow* are not totally different from the usual run of films. The motion picture in America is a product of commercialized culture, dictating and enforcing tastes. It revises the whole character of life. It aids in reconstituting the nature of men. It makes the illusory real, and the real illusory. It has presented a recasted, simplified, and absurd picture of men and women, and of life as it is lived. This is the reason we must dismiss the "Whatever else . . ." formula and why the "occasional" film that is an exception to this average is to be seen as only *occasional*. There is in all this an officialized character to the movie image of life. The movie treatment of everyday life, of personal relationships, is as absurd as is its treatment of history. The general function performed by such films, as I have said, is that of justifying, convincing, and ennobling the status quo. This means that just as leaders must be repositories of all wisdom, so must the masses of the people be healthy, happy, satisfied. If ill befalls them, it must be by their own doing.

In most of these films the average American fares much better than he does in life. His love life in pictures, in particular, is much, much more blissful than it usually is in real life. These motion picture images of life must be rendered acceptable. Entertainment, the reality of trivial details, these usually play the kind of role they do in *Wilson*. Just as personal life is without depth in the ordinary escapist film, so is history without depth in *Wilson*. These historical films with a message are similar in intent to the films that are pure "entertainment" and embody no overt message.

Further, it is pertinent to comment on how time is treated in most films as a means of creating nostalgic emotions. In most films time is established in terms of simple chronology and is expressed symbolically by sound and image. Old-time songs, styles in clothing, the design of vehicles are the most familiar means of registering the passing of time. Besides inducing lethargic moods of lulling nostalgia, this method of registering the passing of time further renders the status quo palatable. In such a way we are told that America was good in the past, too. Life was good in other days. People then usually were as healthy and as happy as those portrayed now by Cary Grant and Lana Turner. Time thus passes in most films as if it were without depth, without depth in the sense that it is a temporal span during which something happens to people living in society. One of the merits of Orson Welles as a producer is that he has treated time with some sense of this depth so uniformly lacking in most films.

III

Let us contrast the sort of film we have been discussing with the early Soviet pictures. In particular, let us contrast these new films with a message with the great Soviet picture, *Ten Days That Shook The World*. *Ten Days That Shook The World* is a pictorial re-creation of an historic event that has had the far-reaching result of affecting the whole future of humanity. The October Revolution was not without its leaders, its Lenin and Trotsky, whose brilliance can scarcely be denied even by their enemies. These men played a far from insignificant role in the events of the Russian Revolution. And yet, consider the treatment of leadership in *Ten Days That Shook The World*. (Here the question of Trotsky is not directly relevant since his role was minimized for official reasons. The leadership as a whole is portrayed functionally and in relationship with the masses.) In this film leaders are portrayed with striking difference from the way they are portrayed in films like *Wilson, Mission to Moscow,* or even the current run of bureaucratized Soviet films. In *Ten Days That Shook The World* the masses are the center, the focus of the film. This demonstrates that there are other patterns, other film possibilities that are not merely theoretical. Under a different social organization we can glimpse a sense of the possibilities of the film as a cultural medium, as an art form. Similar points also can be made about films of individual character and personal relationships. For pictures like *Ten Days That Shook The World* are but one of many kinds of films. In this context, let us ask why this is so. Why is it, for instance, that when *Ten Days That Shook The World* was made (and it was filmed, too, in the period of Stalin's rule) there seems to have been no question as to the necessity of sugar-coating, of entertaining? Is it that the Russian masses, so much more backward than the Americans in some respects, are superior to the masses of the American people? Not at all. The need for profit didn't create the special need for entertainment which seems to be—if one accepts what comes from California—the almighty necessity of millions of Americans. And at that time the needs of the state and of the prevailing system as a whole did not naturally lead to either an escapist film or to a film that was totally bureaucratized and had to close the gap between official explanations and real explanations.

Just as films do not fill the real needs of the masses of the people, just as they do not really perform a mission and play an educative role, so is it that in the films themselves, the consequences of this are revealed. In the films the masses of the people must have false needs—the need of leaders who possess the wisdom of gods as well as a need for an endless entertainment and so on. This is why the real becomes unreal, and the unreal real. And the social consequences of this are incalculable. The motion picture today is having a profound influence on almost all of social life. By and large that influence is expressed in terms of false images of reality.

IV

Mr. Walter Wanger, in an article, "Hollywood and the Intellectual" (the *Saturday Review of Literature*, December 5, 1942), appealed to intellectuals not to take a snobbish attitude toward pictures. He argued that the motion picture has the means of reaching the audiences that liberal intellectuals want to reach. There must be an *entente cordiale* between liberal intellectuals and Hollywood. In the world after the War, he asserted, films will permit the intellectuals to reach the masses. He cited what he called a fictitious instance, that of liberated Poland. He claimed that the effects of Hitler's propaganda in liberated Poland would remain, and would have to be eradicated in order that the four freedoms might be realized. He defended the star system as a means of achieving these aims, arguing that glamorous personalities make truths and ideals concrete. He added that Goebbels would give anything to have Hollywood, but that he could not get it, and that hence Goebbels did not have any glamour with which to surround his propaganda. Hollywood has it in actors who are "regular guys" and its actresses who wear sweaters and "signify sprightly comedy on the screen." And he further insisted: "Recognition is needed that skills do exist in Hollywood, that producers, directors, writers of films are not some tribe apart, but men who have learned the technique of speaking to the world today. Pass over producers and directors. They are merely men who have spent twenty-five or thirty years studying public entertainment standards and how to apply them. . . . A novelist or a playwright writes. Whatever he does is his, not only in monetary reward but in critical appraisal. A scenarist writes. He is scarcely heard of unless some superior blames him for a poor picture. The fact that skill is involved in the writing of screen plays is proved by the records of many authors, competent in other fields, who have failed to make good in Hollywood. . . . We make a face both at posterity and history if we assume that none of this writing is literature."

Here one sees, all over again, the same tendencies in operation. Mr. Wanger is widely recognized as one of the leading liberals of Hollywood. Consider his plea. He appeals to writers, with the assurance that they will find an audience. He urges writers, liberals, and picture-makers to "educate" and lead the masses; they must teach the liberated Poles as well as the never-enslaved Americans how to be free, how to foster ideals. He appeals for recognition of Hollywood on the ground that its picture-makers have the skill and the experience to carry out this program. He argues that some Hollywood writing is literature and will be remembered. Fame, prestige, hero-worship, speaking down to the masses, using girls who embody a sprightly sense of comedy and stars who are "regular guys"—all this is involved in his appeal. One is led to ask a question: Might it not be possible for the masses—who have to be taught by sweater girls and to be entertained—to teach something? Might they not be given a voice? Might they not have lessons to teach? Might it not all be conceived just the other way around? In spite of the men of skill, the men with twenty-five or thirty years of experience in applying standards of entertainment and learning how to coat facts with sugar, is it not possible that all those who are supposed to need pills might not really need them? Might it not even be true that these skilled picture-makers themselves need some of the consoling pills? There have been occasions in history when this has happened. Such occasions may arise again. History, as is well known, is full of surprises, big ones and little ones. Hollywood, aroused to meet the facts of life, is embarking on an allegedly new course. But these facts of life are harder than some people realize. The future will teach us just how hard they are. In the meantime, if we wish to be just tough enough not to be cut by these hard facts, it might possibly be better to reduce the sugar on the pills.

Perhaps there may be the danger of a kind of historical and social diabetes developing in the kind of culture Hollywood is now creating. As Thomas Huxley once remarked, facts are stubborn things. Concerning the hard facts now stirring Hollywood, gentlemen beware: they may be more stubborn than glamour, skill, and experience in the application of entertainment standards. History has been discovered in Beverly Hills and Burbank, California; perhaps history may yet repay its gratitude for that discovery. It may discover these localities. And if it does, there may yet be such a revulsion of taste that all this glamour, all this skill, all this fame may seem a little tawdry.

1944

"This book should help to clear the atmosphere for some time to come."

JOSEPH WARREN BEACH in
The N. Y. Times Book Review

The battle of the books is being resumed on a wider front. Under different terms (and leaders) the controversy that was waged in the thirties over "humanism" is being fought once more.

To this battle and to an understanding of literature and its function in society Mr. Farrell makes a noteworthy contribution in this volume. The critical articles it contains are on diverse subjects but represent a consistent point of view; the evaluations of specific writers serve to illustrate how this point of view is applied. Among the men whose work Mr. Farrell appraises are Joyce, Dostoievsky, Mark Twain, Chekhov, Hemingway, and Ring Lardner.

Many of the papers in this book created widespread discussion when they first appeared in such periodicals as *The Atlantic Monthly*, *The New Republic*, *The New York Times*, *The Saturday Review of Literature*, and *The Nation*.